CATHOLIC TRIVIA

MARK ELVINS

CATHOLIC TRIVIA

....

OUR FORGOTTEN HERITAGE

Illustrated by John Ryan

HARPERCOLLINS RELIGIOUS
An Imprint of HarperCollins*Publishers*

HarperCollins*Religious*
Part of HarperCollins*Publishers*
77–85 Fulham Palace Road
Hammersmith, London W6 8JB

First published in Great Britain
in 1992 by HarperCollins*Religious*

1 3 5 7 9 10 8 6 4 2

ISBN 0 00 599342-3

Printed and bound by Bell and Bain Ltd., Glasgow

Royalties to the St Thomas Fund for the Homeless

CONTENTS

Old Sayings 47

Flowers with Religious Names 129

INTRODUCTION

Catholic Trivia is a humble attempt to list all the sayings, customs and traditions of a Catholic origin, to show how much the Church has affected and still affects our everyday lives. Many of these customs have lost their original religious significance, and often they survive only as mere superstition, such as touching wood or crossing fingers. *A Dictionary of Superstitions* (OUP, 1989) by Iona Opie and Moira Tatem gives plenty of evidence for the ancient and pre-Reformation origins of numerous superstitions, but fails to explain how many had their initial popularity through a religious inspiration. Many of these religious customs have thus become plagiarized by folklorists and been given a secular category, their Catholic origins being long forgotten. The term "folklore" was coined in the last century to describe customs and practices which had survived with obscure or half-remembered origins. *Catholic Trivia* may thus be excused for claiming back some of these social trifles.

Many Catholic customs had a liturgical inspiration associated with religious festivals. Today these festivals have mostly changed, leaving their associate customs misunderstood and disconnected. Old customs have become new superstitions. One reason for this was the massive social and cultural dislocation wrought by the Reformation, and another was the puritanical attitudes of many liturgists of more recent (post-conciliar) times.

A number of interesting reversals have occurred. The spilling of salt, today associated with bad luck, had a Catholic origin, salt being used in the preparation of holy water, the time-

13

honoured protection against the Devil. The number thirteen used to be considered lucky, representing the twelve disciples with Our Lord (hence the baker's dozen), but Puritan extremists reversed the custom to produce the modern superstition of bad luck. When the Revd Henry Bourne wrote his *Antiquitates Vulgares* in 1725 he blamed Catholic monks for introducing "many silly and wicked opinions, to keep the world in Awe and ignorance". Such religious extremists even regarded Christmas as superstitious, and Cromwell in his day actually outlawed the consumption of Christmas pudding and mince pies. In fact the zeal to stamp out popery turned many religious customs into negative superstitions, like walking under ladders (ladders were seen as a symbol of Our Lord's Passion and were walked under to invoke divine protection). The same zeal led to the dropping of the papal tiara in the arms both of the See of York and of the Guild of White Bread Bakers. Winchester scholars used to bow to a statue of Our Lady; the bowing continues but the offending statue has long been removed.

In fact, as religious customs declined real superstition increased in a kind of inverse ratio. The crucifix or St Christopher medal, which was once invoked for divine aid, has now been replaced by a rabbit's foot for good luck. Without the anchor of religion, superstitions, and even occult practices, have become more widespread. Compared with such things, the old Catholic customs described in this book seem quaint, harmless and colourful.

Abbot Horne, FSA, in his preface to the pamphlet *Relics of Popery* (CTS, 1949), sought to record such Catholic trivia, adding that there were probably many more than he had listed. In 1979 I produced *Old Catholic England* (CTS), in which I added a great deal to Abbot Horne's original record. This was in part to remind Catholics of a more flamboyant past rapidly being forgotten. The present text is yet another expansion on the original work. I here record my gratitude to David Murphy of the Catholic Truth Society, who has waived any copyright on *Old Catholic England*. I hope the present edition is as full as can be expected, and will contribute a little whimsy to the dull religious practices of our time. Apart from Abbot Horne, I have drawn extensively upon Opie and Tatem (see above) and *Dr Brewer's Dictionary of Phrase and Fable* (Cassell, 1991, revised). In the main text these sources are identified by the initials *DS* and *BDPF* respectively.

The final section of this book deals with the origin of the title, "Mary's Dowry", given to England at the behest of King Richard II in 1381. The year 1993 is the centenary of the rededication of England as "Mary's Dowry". This was done on 2nd July 1893 at Brompton Oratory by Cardinal Vaughan at the invitation of Pope Leo XIII. (The original dedication in 1381 followed a poll tax revolt which nearly lost King Richard his throne: the recent poll tax has seen history repeat itself.)

All royalties from the sale of *Catholic Trivia* are dedicated to the work of the St Thomas Fund for the Homeless.

DAYS AND SEASONS

The Feast of Fools

A kind of saturnalia popular in the Middle Ages. Its chief object was to honour the ass on which Our Lord made His triumphal journey into Jerusalem. The feast was held on 1st January (the Feast of Circumcision in the old calendar). An ass was an essential feature (some wooden ones still remain, cf. Horniman Museum). Braying replaced the Amen in the fifteenth century.

The Feast of the Conversion of St Paul

This feast was held on 25th January and was famous for rural prophecy. If it was a fine day there would be a good harvest; if the feast day was wet the harvest would be a poor one.

Candlemas

This was the time which coincided with increasing daylight, and so all the old candles could be used up for the feast (2nd February). "Candlemas" was the popular name for the Feast of the Purification of Our Lady of the Presentation of Our Lord. Candles blessed on this day were believed to preserve one from the power of witchcraft: "such as observe duulie the rites and ceremonies of holie church . . . by the lawful use of candles hallowed on Candlemas Daie . . . are preserved from witchcraft" (Scot, *Discoverie of Witchcraft* XII.xx, 1584).

Lady Day

So called after the Feast of the Annunciation on 25th March. It was formerly called "St Mary's Day in Lent" to distinguish it from the other feasts of Our Lady (also called Lady Days). Until 1752 it was this day that marked the beginning of the New Year, and it still remains one of the traditional Quarter Days.

All Fools' Day

When the Feast of the Annunciation was given a full octave, before the Reformation, seven days were kept with great solemnity. However, on the eighth day there was a general relaxation from all the dignified liturgical celebration and an excuse was made for general merriment, particularly in the form of practical jokes. This especially applied to the clerks and minor canons, who took the opportunity of mocking their superiors. The octave day was, of course, 1st April.

Merry Monday (or Blue Monday)

The day before Shrove Tuesday and the onset of Lent. This day, spent in dissipation, was said to leave everything with a bluish tinge through inebriation.

Carnival

A season preceding Lent, devoted to merry-making. Taken from the Latin *carnis*, "flesh", and *levare*, "to remove", the name signified the abstinence from flesh meats after Shrove Tuesday, when Lent begins.

Shrove Tuesday

The name of this day is another link with our Catholic past. To "shrive" or to be "shriven" were the terms our forefathers used concerning the Sacrament of Confession. It was the old custom in this country to prepare for Lent by going to confession on either the Monday or the Tuesday before Ash Wednesday, and hence this time was often called Shrove-tide. A bell is still rung by ancient custom in several of the old parish churches on Shrove Tuesday; the people call it "the Pancake Bell", but it is really the bell that used to call them to church for the Lent confession. Pancakes were eaten on Shrove Tuesday probably because eggs were among the kinds of food not allowed during Lent, or perhaps during those days in Lent when what was called a "black fast" had to be kept. To make pancakes required many eggs, so they were a way of using up eggs.

Lent

This season was introduced by Pope Felix III in the fourth century. Originally it lasted for thirty-six days, but four days were added in 487 to make up the forty days Our Lord spent in the wilderness. The word "Lent" is taken from "Lenctenid", which is Old English for spring-tide and the Saxon name for March because of the lengthening of the days. As Lent falls in March, it is fittingly named.

Fish in Lent

The forty days of Lent were always marked by fasting and abstinence. The abstinence from flesh meats meant that large quantities of fish were eaten instead. In the thirty-first year of the reign of Edward III the Exchequer records the following sums paid for fish consumed by the royal household during Lent: "Fifty marks for five lasts [9,000] of red herrings, twelve pounds for two lasts of white herrings, six pounds for two barrels of sturgeon, twenty-one pounds five shillings for 1,300 stock-fish, thirteen shillings and nine pence for eighty-nine congers, twenty marks for three hundred and twenty mulwells."

Fish was *de rigueur* during Lent and any who wished to take meat could only do so on account of bodily infirmity. In these cases the clergy would grant a licence for the consumption of flesh meat. Moreover, payment was often made to this end. In the parish record of St Martin's, Ontwich, in the year 1525 we read, "Received of the Lady Atham for the use of the poore, for license to eat flesh £0.13s.4d." In the parish of St Mary's, Leicester, a licence was granted to Lady Barbara Hastings to eat meat in Lent, on account of her great age.

Those who broke the laws of abstinence were frequently confined to pillory or stocks and made a public example. The laws were continued by Elizabeth I, as much to support the fish trade as to continue pious tradition. These were enforced by a 1548 Act of Parliament which imposed a penalty of ten shillings and ten days' imprisonment on any backsliders (twenty shillings and twenty days' imprisonment if the offence was repeated).

James II in 1687 inserted in the *London Gazette* a proclamation

enjoining abstinence from meat during Lent, but licences for meat-eating could be obtained from the office in St Paul's Churchyard. A year later James abdicated and the statute regarding Lenten fare became a dead letter, being repealed in 1863 by the Statute Law Revision Act. The custom, however, remains as part of Roman Canon law, in particular for Ash Wednesday and Good Friday, the other days of Lent being left to individual conscience (cf. William Andrews, FRHS, *Curiosities of the Church*, London, 1890).

A "fish day" was a day when it was forbidden to eat flesh meats. Thus all Fridays, Ember days (q.v.), Ash Wednesday, Wednesdays in Lent and the vigils of Pentecost, the Assumption, All Saints and Christmas were "fish days".

Laetare Sunday (or Mothering Sunday)

The fourth Sunday in Lent, so named from the opening words of the Entrance Antiphon at Mass ("Rejoice Jerusalem", Isaiah 66:10). Certain relaxations are permitted on this day, despite the penitential season, such as the wearing of rose-pink vestments. (Such vestments are also permitted on Gaudete Sunday (also named from the opening words of the Mass), the third Sunday in Advent.) On Laetare Sunday the Pope blesses the golden roses. This day is also called Refreshment Sunday, because the Gospel used to be the feeding of the five thousand (John 6:1–15), and it was the day simnel cakes were eaten as a relaxation from Lenten rigour. The fourth Sunday in Lent is also called Mothering Sunday; this refers to the custom of visiting the local cathedral or mother church, or, in some parts of England, one's mother. The tradition has grown out of the words which used to occur in the epistle of the day, "Jerusalem . . . which is the mother of us all" (Galatians 4:26). "Mother's Day" is an invention of commercial card manufacturers. The bringing of flowers to the senior mother of the family (the grandmother) may also associate "Little Red Riding Hood", who brought flowers to her grandmother.

Care Sunday

The fifth Sunday in Lent. "Care" here means suffering, taken from the old High German "Kar-fritag" in reference to the sufferings of Christ. The other name is Passion Sunday (now combined with Palm Sunday). An alternative name is "Carling Sunday": in the north of England it was customary on this day to eat parched peas fried in butter, called "carlings".

Palm Sunday

On this day, the Sunday before Easter, palms are blessed and distributed to the congregation, in memory of Our Lord's ride into Jerusalem, when the people broke off boughs from trees and strewed them on the road before Him (John 12:12–19). In this country the old name "palm" has clung to the willow, with its golden or silver catkins which show in the early spring. There can be no doubt that these catkin-covered willows were carried by our forefathers on Palm Sunday, when Easter fell at a time when the willow could be used. But when an early or very late Easter made the use of this kind of palm impossible, yew from the churchyard was carried instead. In parts of Kent the yew is still called a "palm". The quiet little graveyard on the south side of Wells Cathedral is known as the "Palm churchyard". In the middle of it stands a very ancient yew tree. Throughout rural Ireland the churchyard yew is always spoken of as the "Palm tree", and pieces from it are used on Palm Sunday.

23

Friday

This day is popularly associated with bad luck, probably on the grounds that Our Lord was crucified on a Friday, e.g. "And on a Friday fil al this meschaunce" (Chaucer, "Nun's Priest Tale", 1390). (*DS*)

Spy Wednesday

A name given in Ireland to the Wednesday before Good Friday, when Judas bargained to become the spy of the Jewish Sanhedrin (Matthew 26:3–5, 14–16).

Maundy Thursday

The Thursday following Palm Sunday, or the day before Good Friday, still goes by this name. The Maundy, in Catholic England, meant the reigning sovereign washing the feet of a certain number of poor men on this day. For centuries the ceremony took place in Westminster Abbey. The word "Maundy" comes from the first Latin word in this ceremony (Introit), *Mandatum*, and it is a reference to Our Lord's statement that He was giving a new command to the disciples when He carried out the ceremony of washing their feet (John 13). Although the royal ceremony of the washing of feet has been given up since the Reformation, the conclusion of that ceremony, where each of the poor men was given a gift of money, is still kept up. Each recipient has a purse of new coins given him which are specially minted for the occasion. Hence what is known as the "Royal Maundy" is a very real survival of a remnant of the old religion. After the original ceremony the poor men were given a meal and the sovereign would wait on his guests at table.

Good Friday and hot cross buns

It is somewhat doubtful whether hot cross buns were provided in pre-Reformation days, as no direct evidence to that effect can be found. On the other hand, it is unlikely that they were introduced by Puritans, who disliked the sign of the cross and condemned special foods that were customary at particular seasons. As early fasting laws forbade the use of milk and butter on certain days, it seems probable that a plain kind of bread may

25

have been sold on Good Friday, made without the forbidden ingredients, and hot cross buns may be its descendant. Our English Good Friday buns were originally quite plain, with perhaps a little spice added to them. It was not until about 1840 that currants first appeared in them.

Easter Sunday and Easter Cakes

Easter cakes – a sort of large biscuit flavoured with cinnamon – are made in many parts of the west country at Easter time. They were frequently sold at the church door by the sacristan (or sexton, as he was more often called) and were doubtless bought by those who had come a long way to make their Easter Communion, and hence would be fasting. The Easter cake would help them on their walk home again.

Hock-day (or Hock Tuesday)

This was the second Tuesday after Easter and was long held as a festival in England. It was the time for paying church dues, and landlords received an annual tribute ("hock money") for allowing tenants and serfs to commemorate the day. "Hoke Monday was for the men and Hoke Tuesday for the women. On both days the men and women alternately, with great merriment, obstructed the public road with ropes, and pulled passengers to them, from Julian they exacted money to be laid out in pious uses" (Brand, *Antiquities* Vol. I, p. 187).

Easter eggs

In mediaeval times eggs were forbidden during the forty days of Lenten fasting. Thus the first eggs after Lent were those consumed on Easter Sunday; these eggs signified Christ's coming from the tomb and the new life of Easter.

Quasimodo Sunday (or Low Sunday)

The first Sunday after Easter, called after the Introit of the day: *Quasimodo geniti infantes* ("as new-born babes", 1 Peter 11:2). This Sunday was the presumed birthday of the hunchback of Notre Dame.

Corpus Christi and the procession of the Blessed Sacrament

The old village benefit clubs have now nearly ceased to exist, as the National Insurance Acts (1948 onwards) killed most of them. Many of these clubs must have dated back to Catholic times, for not a few kept the annual feast or meeting-day on what is now called Trinity Thursday, which is, of course, the Feast of Corpus Christi. The benefit club would have joined in the procession of the Blessed Sacrament on that day, which was a holiday, and so the members would have been free to carry out their business meeting afterwards, at which they settled the financial affairs of their club. In Sutri, outside Rome, a carpet of flowers is laid for the procession of the Blessed Sacrament, and in 1877 this custom was introduced to Arundel by the fifteenth Duke of Norfolk. The feast is kept on the first free Thursday after Easter, to celebrate with greater festivity the institution of the Blessed Sacrament. Maundy Thursday, being in Lent, is restricted from such celebration.

Cantate Sunday

This is another name for Rogation Sunday (the fourth after Easter). Cantate Sunday was named after the first word of the Introit of the Mass, *Cantate Domino* ("Sing to the Lord"). Now the Introit is *Misericordia Domini*.

The Rogation Days

The three days before the Feast of Our Lord's Ascension were known as the Rogation Days, and the Litanies of the Saints were sung in procession on these days. What was known as "beating the bounds" consisted in walking round the boundaries of the parish so that they might be clearly defined and so that the obligation of supporting the poor in the parish might have its just limits. Advantage was taken of the Rogation procession in times past for defining parish boundaries. Although these processions were suppressed in 1547, Elizabeth I in 1559 ordered a perambulation of the parish instead. We still have a remnant of this in the custom of beating the bounds, which goes on in places here and there around the time of the Feast of the Ascension.

Chadpence

The Whitsuntide offerings at Lichfield Cathedral, dedicated to the upkeep of the building, whose patron is St Chad.

The May ceremonies and their origins

In an age when so many old customs have become the preserve of folk museums, some of the more spectacular ones have lately experienced a spirited but rather self-conscious revival. Where such ceremonies retain some of their ancient natural vigour, it is because they have largely become the property of children. The May ceremonies have thus survived in a vestigial form as the result of continuing youthful enthusiasm.

The origins of these ceremonies can be traced back to ancient Rome and the pagan festival of the goddess Flora, which commemorated the return of spring in the renewed fertility of vegetation. Today the tradition of gathering spring flowers is enjoyed for its own sake. People come back to town with armfuls of bluebells, primroses and cowslips ("May flowers") perpetuating the custom of "gathering in May". Until fairly recent times the custom was widespread in Western Europe.

Indeed, the seventeenth-century poet, Robert Herrick, could write:

There's not a budding Boy or Girl this day
But is got up and gone to bring in May.

The garland for the Queen of the May was an essential element in the rites of May, for the maiden chosen represented the return of spring and was crowned with flowers in an act of homage to the goddess of springtime. It is plain that the ancient goddess Flora has thus continued in folklore in a modified form as the May Queen.

In the Middle Ages the Church felt obliged to give this harmless but obviously pagan custom a Christian guise. Where pre-Christian customs had become firmly established, the Church would seek to introduce a Christian context, although the devotions were of a popular rather than an official nature. By the thirteenth century Christian May ceremonies had become well established, and in the fourteenth century Blessed Henry Suso, a German Dominican friar, could write of "fetching in the May", once for Christ and twice for "the tender flower and Rosy Maid, the Mother of God". He also mentions in his autobiography the May custom of making a little "chaplet" or garland of roses to crown a statue of the Virgin Mary. The chaplet of roses was a love token well known in the Middle Ages. Indeed, knights would risk their lives jousting to win a lady's favour; the victorious knight would be given the honour of crowning "the Queen of the Tournament" with this garland. This piece of colourful chivalry readily lent itself to popular international devotion to the Virgin Mary. It is from this association that the prayer beads came to be called rosary beads, and being described as a chaplet, they were originally carved in the shape of roses.

These Christian devotions continued, however, alongside the older, pre-Christian customs. Henry VIII would regularly ride his court down to Kent to keep the May ceremonies, and on one occasion Queen Anne Boleyn was crowned Queen of the May. Moreover, in some instances the May Queen was named "Maid Marion", a corruption of "Mary", showing the connection with the Blessed Virgin. In many English villages the May Queen came to be called the "May Lady", and until quite recently the children of the little village of Charlton-upon-Otmoor in Oxfordshire would go from door to door asking for "flowers for the Lady", presumably to make her garland.

Many of the old May ceremonies were, of course, stamped out by the Puritans of the seventeenth century, but in some country parts such as Charlton-upon-Otmoor they persisted. In Hereford in 1887 every doorway is recorded as being decorated with green birch, and in Abney, Derbyshire, in 1901, "a garland hung above every door". The garlands retained their significance as love tokens, but in Catholic Lancashire "Garland Sunday" (the first Sunday in May) retained its religious flavour also.

In conclusion, no discourse on May ceremonies would be complete without mention of the continuing and very popular May ceremonies at Oxford, where at six o'clock on the morning of 1st May a Latin May carol is sung from the top of Magdalen College Tower, while down below young people congregate with their garlands of May.

May devotions in their present form originated in Rome at the end of the eighteenth century, where Father Latomia of the Roman Jesuit College, in order to counteract the infidelity and immorality that he found among the students, made a vow to devote the month of May to Mary. The devotions in this college spread to other Jesuit schools, and from them they were taken on in various countries. May devotions were restored in England by

Father Gentili, the Italian Father of Charity, who was doing such wonderful work in this country between 1840 and 1850.

May Day as a public holiday and dancing round the Maypole were certainly very old customs, and many pre-Reformation poets, Chaucer in particular, have written in praise of the month of May.

The birthday of John the Baptist

According to several of the Latin Fathers, John the Baptist was endowed with pre-natal grace at the time of Our Lady's Visitation (Luke 1:41) to his mother, St Elizabeth. Consequently his birthday was originally celebrated in connection with the Epiphany, but from the fourth century this was fixed on 24th June (six months after Christmas). The liturgy of the Feast has retained certain affinities with that of Christmas, but whereas Christmas occupies the approximate time of the winter solstice, the Feast of John the Baptist is fixed at the time of the summer solstice (midsummer). The association with Christmas has, moreover, resulted in a curiously unofficial commemoration of the ass which was present at Our Lord's nativity and took the Holy Family into Egypt. Being left out of the Christmas celebrations, the ass was sometimes remembered at midsummer instead. This is demonstrated in Shakespeare's *Midsummer Night's Dream* when the character Bottom is given the head of an ass. The ass, of course, is also famous for the cross on its back, which is seen as commemorating Our Saviour's ride into Jerusalem.

St Swithin's Day

This occurs traditionally on 15th July; if it is a wet day, this is supposed to presage forty days of rain. St Swithin (d. 862,

Bishop of Winchester), who disliked pomp, brought this retribution when his remains were removed from a common graveyard to Winchester Cathedral on 15th July. The monks, faced with forty days of rain, concluded that their saint had caused this rainy period in order to show his disapproval. His shrine was destroyed at the Reformation. "St Swithin's day gif ye to rain, for forty days it will remain: St Swithin's day, an ye be fair, for forty twill rain nae mair." (DS)

St James' grotto

The Feast of St James the Great of Compostella used to be celebrated on 5th August, but since the change to the Gregorian Calendar in 1752, it has been celebrated on 25th July. The scallop shell was the badge of this saint and Apostle, as borne by the pilgrims to his shrine at Compostella in Spain. The old custom of children building grottoes of shells on 5th August continued up until modern times. As late as 1944 a writer to *The Times* spotted such a grotto under the arches at Finsbury Park Station. The grottoes, built from oyster shells (thus Whitstable was a place to see them at one time), were topped with a lighted candle and were displayed at street corners. The children would ask the passer-by, "Please remember the grotto", and by giving a penny the candle could be kept alight. This custom originated in Catholic England as a means of raising money for poor pilgrims seeking the boat fare to Compostella.

> *And how should I know your true love*
> *From many other one?*
> *Oh by his scallop shell and hat*
> *And by his sandal shoon.*
>
> Friar of Orders Grey

Lammas Day

The word "Lammas" is to be found in a work by King Alfred and was in common use throughout the Middle Ages. It is derived from the two words "loaf" and "Mass" and was used to describe the first day of August, when the bread to be consecrated at Mass was taken from the first ripe corn. Thus this day was an early form of Harvest Thanksgiving.

Holy Rood Day

Holy Rood Day or Holy Cross Day (14th September) was not a day on which to go gathering nuts, as many had met the Devil doing the same on this day (Holy Rood Day was said to be the day "when the Devil goes a-nutting"). The same rule also applied to all Sundays – this was a caution to keep Sundays holy. (*DS*)

Michaelmas

The Feast of St Michael the Archangel (now united with Gabriel and Raphael) is celebrated on 29th September. This feast came at the end of harvesting, when livestock was calculated and fodder was arranged for the winter. Thus this was a time of animal fairs, and the Michaelmas goose became a custom. Michaelmas also gives its name to a Law term together with Easter, Trinity and Hilary, names which bespeak their Christian origins (cf. Univerity terms).

The Feast of St Simon and St Jude

In mediaeval England this day (28th October) usually marked the beginning of winter, for by the end of October the fine weather is usually replaced by winter gales (*Folklore Myths and Legends of Britain*, Reader's Digest Association, London, 1973).

Bonfires

Originally "bonefires". "In some parts of Lincolnshire . . . they make fires in the public streets . . . with bones of oxen, sheep etc. . . . hence came the origin of bon-fires" (Leland, 1552). A combination of wood and bones "is called St John's fire", as these were burnt on the feast of St John (27th December). (Wynkyn de Worde, *Festyvall*, 1493.)

Bonfire Night

In most parts of the country the night of 5th November provides a perfect excuse for lighting bonfires and indulging in respectable merriment. Indeed, the observation of this day was made legally enforceable by Act of Parliament in 1605, during the third year of the reign of James I. To this was added in the Anglican Book of Common Prayer a service of commemoration, to be used annually on this day, by proclamation (revoked in 1859).

Although the celebrations are harmless enough, the event that inspired this tradition was a dark and sinister plot, surrounded by so much treachery and intrigue that perhaps the full truth will never be known. It is popularly believed that the "Gunpowder Plot" was a plan by a few Catholic gentlemen to blow up the Houses of Parliament. However, recent research has shown that Robert Cecil, King James' Principal Secretary, could have engineered the whole business to further his own political career.

Suffice it to say that the supposed culprits, whether duped into compromising their struggle for political freedom or not, were speedily brought to justice. Their ring-leader, Guy Fawkes, has been annually burnt in effigy ever since.

But the tradition of Bonfire Night, although it may seem to derive from the sectarian bitterness of the seventeenth century, is in fact part of an old custom dating back to pre-Christian times. During the Celtic "fire festival" of Samain bonfires were lit: the purpose of this was to strengthen the winter sun. Moreover, 31st October in the old Celtic calendar was New Year's Eve. On this day the dead were commemorated, and it was believed that spirits then walked abroad and the dead returned to earth. At this time all fires were extinguished, to be rekindled later from the many bonfires that were lit to welcome returning spirits.

These traditions became so deeply rooted in local custom that the Church was forced to compromise by establishing in 837 the Feast of All Saints on 1st November, and the Commemoration of All Souls on 2nd November. It was in fact the practice of the Christian missionaries throughout Europe to absorb pagan customs and Christianize them. Since Britain and Ireland were considered to be separate from Europe at this time they had a separate calendar in which all the Irish and British saints were celebrated on 1st November. It was from the British Isles that the keeping of All Saints on this day gradually spread to the rest of Christendom. (*New Catholic Encyclopaedia* Vol. 1, New York, 1967, p. 318.)

Thus the bonfires that were lit to welcome the returning spirits were transferred from Hallowe'en to the night of 1st November. Bonfire Night as kept today thus has not only a Celtic pagan origin, but also an association with the Church's calendar, which makes the unfortunate Guy Fawkes seem a bit of an interloper. However, in the north of England the old traditional Bonfire

Night, as practised on 1st November, persisted well into the nineteenth century.

Martinmas

The Feast of St Martin of Tours (11th November) marked the end of the season of bonfires and the slaughtering of beasts for the winter. It was also a time of great feasting. If the sun returned with a spasm of summer heat, as on occasion it did at this time, it was called St Martin's Summer (cf. St Luke's Summer, 15th October). (Violet Alford, *An Introduction to English Folklore*, Bell & Sons, London, 1952.)

The Feast of St Nicholas, Holy Innocents' Day and "boy bishops"

The custom of electing "boy bishops" on the Feast of St Nicholas (6th December) was one of the most popular traditions in England before the Reformation. The boy bishop took office on 6th December, and his authority lasted until Holy Innocents' Day (28th December). St Nicholas was the patron saint of children. Nicholas, moreover, was considered the special patron of choirboys, and his festival began a season of boyish merriment. Deans and canons would join in wholeheartedly (the festivities were largely confined to cathedral parishes), proving that ecclesiastical dignitaries could enjoy themselves when the occasion demanded.

In fact, so popular did this picturesque custom become that boy bishops were elected not only in cathedrals, but also in collegiate churches, colleges and grammar schools (Eton elected two!) and in almost every parish.

One of the main ideas behind the election of boy bishops was

to impress upon children the honour and dignity of the priesthood, and the young bishop was held in deep veneration not only by children but by adults as well. So sacred was the office considered to be that according to the Statute of Sarum no one was to interrupt when a boy bishop was officiating, upon pain of anathema. If he died during his tenure he was buried with full ceremony in all his pontifical vestments, and a monument was erected to his memory, together with his episcopal effigy.

About three hundred years ago, when this custom was almost forgotten, a boy bishop's memorial was discovered in Salisbury Cathedral under the seats near the pulpit. This diminutive effigy in stone is now in the north aisle of the nave. The boy is in full episcopal robes, and has his foot on a lion-headed and dragon-

41

tailed monster – an allusion to the expression of the Psalmist, "Thou shalt tread on the lion and the dragon."

In West Wittering Church, near Chichester, there is a tomb of a boy bishop who is believed to have died in office. The top of it, with a pastoral staff and cross, was found upside down, being used as a paving-stone. It is possible that this was done at a time when mediaeval observances had fallen into disfavour, by a later generation who wished to obliterate their memory.

That the custom under discussion was once popular is proved by the fact that in 1299 Edward I, on his way to Scotland, allowed a boy bishop to say vespers before him in his chapel at Heaton near Newcastle upon Tyne, on the day after his election to the office. The monarch gave him a handsome present as a reward for his services.

From rubrics concerning the processions at Salisbury Cathedral much can be learnt of what happened when the choirboys chose one of their number to be bishop for that year. He was dressed in rich episcopal robes, wore a mitre, and carried a crozier. Two of his companions were elected chaplains, while the rest assumed the character and dress of priests, yielding him canonical obedience. The boy bishop took over the building and, except for Mass, performed the ceremonies and offices.

On the days of celebration the boy bishop and his fellow "clergy", wearing copes and with lighted tapers in their hands, walked in solemn procession to the chancel. The dean and the canons of the cathedral church went first, the chaplains came next, and the boy bishop with his "priests" followed in the last and most honoured place. When the procession reached the chancel the boy bishop went to his throne, and the rest of the youthful "clergy" took their places on either side of him. The residentiary canons, entering into the spirit of the service, carried incense and the Book, and the minor canons had lighted tapers.

Details of the robes used in the ceremony of the boy bishop in the splendid church of St Peter Mancroft, Norwich, have survived. There were four red and white copes; "a cope for the boy who is bishop, paned yellow and blue"; a complete vestment for "my lord and two of his boys"; a vestment "of checker work of green and yellow for the priest to sing in on Saint Nicholas' Day". There were also mitres of painted leather and silvered parchment, and a crozier with a head of gilded timber bearing an image of St Nicholas, for the use of the young bishop.

One is not surprised to learn that this custom was so popular – with parents, boys and the public generally – that it was not easy to suppress. It was banned by Henry VIII in 1542, but it was revived by Queen Mary. Hugh Rhodes, a Master of the Chapels Royal, published a poem with this title: "The song of the Chyld-Bysshop, as it was sung before the Queen's Maiestie in her privie chamber at her mannor of Saint James in the feeldes on Saynt Nicholas's Day and Innocent's Day this yeare now present by chylde bishoppe of Paules church with his company." The Statutes of the famous Dean Colet (he devoted his fortune to re-founding and endowing St Paul's School) order that "all the children shall every Childermas (Innocents' Day) come to Paul's Church, and heare the chylde bishop sermon and after High Mass and each of them offer 1d. to the chylde bishop".

The Feast of Kings

The Epiphany commemorating the arrival of the three Magi (or Kings) bearing their gifts to Bethlehem. It is celebrated on 6th January, when presents were given in the Middle Ages and still are in some countries.

Christmas and mince pies

Today Christmas mince pies are round in shape, but in former times they were oblong. In his *Table Talk* (London, 1689) Selden (d. 1654) says: "The coffin of our Christmas-Pies, in shape long, is in imitation of the Cratch" (manger). In 1644 the Puritan Parliament forbade the observance of Christmas. Soldiers were ordered to break into houses to see that no food such as was formerly eaten at Christmas was used. Plum pudding and mince pies were amongst the forbidden foods.

Robin Redbreast

Although associated with Christmas, this little bird is more appropriate for Good Friday (q.v.). The tradition is that when Our Lord was on His way to Calvary, a robin picked a thorn out of His crown, and His blood on the thorn dyed its breast red. (*BDPF*)

Carols

One tradition claims that the word "carol" is derived from the name of Charlemagne, founder of the Holy Roman Empire.

Another claims that it derives from the old French *carole*, meaning a kind of dance, or the song which accompanied it. Thus the name was applied to the light, joyous hymns which were first sung at Christmas by wandering minstrels. The earliest extant English carol dates from the thirteenth century:

> *Lordlings, listen to our lay*
> *We have come from far away to seek Christmas;*
> *In this mansion we are told*
> *He his yearly feast doth hold.*

Wynkyn de Worde produced the first printed collection of carols in 1521.

Plough Monday

The first Monday after the twelfth day of Christmas, so called because it was the end of the Christmas holidays and marked for many in mediaeval times a return to their work with the plough. It was customary on this day to have ploughs blessed in preparation for seed-time (*The Times*, 10/1/87). Lords of the manor would give a feast before the return to work. The Lord Mayor of London still keeps the "Plough Monday Dinner", when he entertains servants of the Corporation of London.

OLD SAYINGS

"He hasn't a halfpenny to bless himself with"

To bless oneself is to make the sign of the cross, and the saying refers to the old pious custom of a person doing this with the first piece of money he received that day. The recipient crossed himself with the coin, before putting it into his pocket. To give some idea of how very poor a certain man might be, it was enough to say that he did not possess a halfpenny with which to cross himself. After the change in religion, this custom was given up, and the recipient spat upon the coin before putting it into his pocket, and generally said that he did this for luck.

To go "a-roaming"

Or, more accurately, to go "a-Roming" – a term that entered the English language as a consequence of the English love of going to Rome on pilgrimage. Bede records that eight Anglo-Saxon kings abdicated to live as pilgrims in the eternal city.

"Sent to Coventry"

In the fourteenth century unruly members of the Cistercian Order were sent to occupy cells in Coventry to cool off, where in isolation they regained their composure. (*Catholic Herald*, 9/6/89; cf. findings of Margaret Rylatt, Coventry City archaeologist.)

"Tawdry"

A corruption of "St Audrey", "Audrey" being in turn a corruption of "Etheldrida", the name of the patron saint of Ely (cf. St Etheldrida's, Ely Place, London). At the annual fare of St Audrey on the Isle of Ely cheap jewellery and lace was sold; hence "tawdry" came to mean "cheap and shoddy". Shakespeare writes: "Come, you promised me a tawdry lace and a pair of sweet gloves" (*Winter's Tale* IV.iv).

"Red-letter day"

A day of good fortune. Great feasts and Saints' days were always marked in red in the Church's calendar.

"Robbing Peter to pay Paul"

Edward VI endowed St Paul's Cathedral with the manor of Paddington, which he had first taken from the Abbey of St Peter at Westminster.

"When in Rome do as the Romans do"

To conform to local custom. Originally this was a saying of St Ambrose: "When I am in Rome I do as the Romans do", as opposed to "When I am at Milan . . ." (Epistle XXXVI, cf. Kings v:18).

"Salt on the tail"

Blessed salt was (and still is) used in the preparation of holy water. It was also employed to ward off evil (viz. the Devil), and salt on the tail was a remedy against demonic intrusion.

"(God) speed the plough"

A wish for success in some undertaking. This expression occurs in the fifteenth-century song "Plough Monday" (q.v.).

To "laugh up one's sleeve"

This expression probably has a monastic origin. The large choir dress, worn over the religious habit, had voluminous sleeves. When some amusing episode occurred in the monastic choir, such as a ridiculous mistake being made by a novice when reading something, or an absurd blunder being committed when some simple act had to be done, the large sleeves covering the hands made a convenient place in which to bury a laughing face. As the covering of the face in this way was often adopted in private prayer with the object of shutting out distractions, it was not always easy for an onlooker to say for what purpose the sleeve was being used. Hence to "laugh up one's sleeve" became a handy metaphor to describe quiet, unobtrusive laughter.

"Fingers crossed"

Making the sign of the cross to avert bad luck.

Vox populi

The full quote is *vox populi vox Dei*, meaning "the voice of the people is the voice of God". After Edward II had been dethroned by the people in favour of his son Edward III, Walter Reynolds, Archbishop of Canterbury (d. 1327), preached with these words.

"Short shrift"

This saying is still often used, when but little time is allowed to carry something out. It has its origins in the old Anglo-Saxon word, to "shrive", meaning to go to confession and receive absolution. When a criminal was going to be executed he was allowed just time enough to make his confession and receive absolution, before he died. Hence the origin of the expression.

"The mills of God grind slowly"

This expression means that although retribution may be delayed, it is sure to overtake the wicked. It comes from the *Adages* of Erasmus: *Sero molunt deorim moloe*. The full quote is "The mills of God grind slowly, yet they grind exceeding small."

"The weakest must go to the wall"

Many of our old pre-Reformation churches have built into their walls stone benches or seats running down each side of the nave. These seats date from a time before there were any wooden seats filling the nave, and hence the congregation stood throughout Mass, kneeling on the floor at the more solemn moments. Old people and those not in good health naturally found this standing up rather trying, and so they made for the stone benches projecting from the walls. It is easy to see from this how the saying, "The weakest must go to the wall" arose. A fine example of the seats remains in the Hospitaller Church of St John's, Clerkenwell. Stone benches are also to be found around the walls of the churches at St Piran, Minster and Tintagel in Cornwall, and at Bishopstone and Bratton in Wiltshire. There are also examples in Cheshire, Somerset, Derbyshire, Norfolk, Northamptonshire and Yorkshire.

"Bloody"

A popular oath that is really a contraction of "by Our Lady".

"Devil take the hindmost"

This expression derives from mediaeval magic. It was said that the Devil had a school at Toledo or Salamanca, where students, after a certain stage in their studies, had to run through a subterranean passage – the last man being seized by the Devil. (*BDPF*)

To "kick the bucket"

This may not be a very sympathetic or feeling way to describe somebody's death, but the phrase has its origin in an old Catholic custom. After death, when the body had been laid out, a cross and two lighted candles were placed near it. In addition the holy water bucket was brought from the church and put at the feet of the corpse. When friends came to pray for the deceased, before leaving the room they would sprinkle the body with holy water. So intimately, therefore, was the bucket associated with the feet of deceased persons, that it is easy to see how such a saying as to "kick the bucket" came about. Many other explanations of this saying have been given by persons who are unacquainted with Catholic custom.

Dies non

A legal term meaning a day when courts did not sit and no legal business was transacted. Within this category were Sundays and feasts such as Candlemas, Ascension, St John the Baptist, All Saints and the Commemoration of All Souls. The full Latin term was *dies non juridicus* – a non-judicial day.

"Candlemas, candle less"

This saying seems to be confined to the West Country, and it obviously means that as the daylight begins to increase about the beginning of February (Candlemas, 2nd February), so fewer candles are needed for light in the house.

The Doctors' Commons

A locality near St Paul's where the Catholic Ecclesiastical Courts were held and where wills were preserved and marriage licences were granted. It was so called because doctors of law had a "common" table and had to dine together for four days of each law term.

The "thieves' litany"

The cloth trade in Halifax flourished from an early period and contributed greatly to England's economy. Henry I once asked the clothiers of England what boon he could grant them, and one of the Halifax clothiers asked "That whatsoever he was that was taken stealing their Cloth he might presently without any further trial be hanged up." He also asked that the mode of execution be the "Halifax Gibbet", a kind of guillotine devised by a "fat frier". The law thus ordained that any person who stole cloth above the value of thirteen and a half pence would suffer the consequences. This ruling inspired what has been called the "thieves' litany":

> From Hell, Hull and Halifax,
> Good Lord, deliver us.

The gibbet was last used in 1650. Hull was mentioned in the rhyme because of the severity of the law against vagrants in that town.

To canter

This word is taken from the term "Canterbury gallop", which described the ambling pace of the mounts of the Canterbury pilgrims.

"Heresy and hops"

There is a tradition that the hops gardens at Little Chart in Kent were the first to be planted in England, about 1542, the hops being brought from Flanders. Ale was flavoured with various herbs from the earliest times, but it seems that beer was not flavoured with hops until the middle of the sixteenth century. Thus it was said that "Heresy and hops came in together", or as some rhymester has put it:

> *Hops, reformation, baize and beer*
> *Came into England all in a year.*

"Baize" is described by Lipson in his *Economic History of England* (Vol I, p. 435) as an outlandish commodity. Another ballad, in rejecting beer, states that "the old Catholic drink is a pot of good ale".

"When Adam delved"

> *When Adam delved and Eve span,*
> *Who was then the gentleman?*

According to the *Historia Anglicana* of Thomas Walsingham (d. 1422), this was the text of John Ball's speech at Blackheath to Wat Tyler's rebels (1381). The lines were taken from Richard Rolle of Hampole (d. c. 1349). (*BDPF*)

"Adam's apple"

The protruding larynx of men was nicknamed "Adam's apple" to signify a piece of apple stuck in Adam's throat which caused him to choke after taking the forbidden fruit. There is no reference to an apple in Holy Writ – it is a mediaeval Latin play on

words (*malus* = "apple", *mallus* = "evil"), first portrayed in the glass at Chartres Cathedral.

"A little bird told me"

From Ecclesiastes 10:20: "for a bird of the air will carry your voice, or some winged creature tell the matter".

"Third time lucky"

This expression is an obvious reference to the Holy Trinity. It has some obvious parallels, such as the wording of the baptism ceremony and the doffing of hats three times on the introduction of a new peer to the House of Lords.

To "quarrel over the bishop's cope"

To quarrel over something that can't do any good. A bishop of Bruges gave his cope to his people, and they tried to pass it among themselves, thus tearing it to shreds. (*BDPF*)

"All my eye and Betty Martin"

St Martin of Tours was the patron saint of soldiers. *O me Beati Martin* (Latin) or "O my Blessed Martin" could well be the origin of the First World War expression of the British Tommy, "All my eye and Betty Martin". Cf. Oliver Goldsmith in *Good-natured Man* (iii), where the bailiff uses the expression.

Si quis

A notice to whom it may concern given in the parish church before ordination, so that anyone knowing any just cause of impediment may declare the same to the bishop (*si quis* = "if anyone").

"The Clink"

The mediaeval Diocese of Winchester stretched as far as the Thames. Indeed, the bishops had a palace in Clink Street, Southwark, close to a prison they governed. Consequently "the Clink" is now a nickname for all prisons.

"Hocus pocus"

A parody of the words of consecration in the Mass, *Hoc est corpus* (cf. "hoax"). It is a phrase often used by conjurors.

"High Church"

A nineteenth-century expression originally used of Ultra-montanists (i.e. extreme papalists).

"Abracadabra"

A cabalistic charm made up from the initial letters of the Hebrew words *Abba* ("Father"), *Ben* ("Son") and *Ruach* ("Holy Spirit"). It was written out and hung from the neck as an antidote to ague, flux and toothache. (*BDPF*)

"No penny, no paternoster"

No pay, no work, with reference to priests before the Reformation, when a Mass stipend or a stole fee ensured their performance.

NAMES AND TITLES

Father

In the early Church this form of address was given to bishops as teachers; later it became exclusive to clergy who were religious, the seculars being called "Mister", as is still the custom in Ushaw College. To this day the distinction should still apply when addressing clergy on an envelope: "The Rev. N." for a secular and "The Rev. Fr N." for a religious, although few now adhere to this custom. It was Cardinal Manning who introduced the title for all Catholic clergy in spoken address, although now, like the Roman collar, it has been adopted by most other clergy.

Rent days

The old custom of dating events by Saints' days went on right up to the Reformation, after which the Protestants dated events in the modern way (e.g. 24th June). Yet many of the old Catholic titles for feasts still remain. Thus we still have Christmas, Candlemas (2nd February, when rents are still paid in the West Country), Michaelmas, Martinmas and several more; Lady Day (the Feast of Our Blessed Lady, 25th March being her Annunciation) is one of the well-known quarter days, together with Midsummer Day (24th June), Michaelmas (29th September) and Christmas Day, when quarterly rents were due for payment. There is evidence that the Reformers tried to get rid of these old popish names, and they spoke of Christtide,

Michaeltide etc., but these new names never became popular, and we still have those used by our Catholic forefathers.

Titles

In some cases old Catholic titles have continued where we should least expect them. The names of the Sees in the Established Church are mostly those that were in use before the Reformation. Thus we have, "Cantuar", "Ebor", "Londin" etc. (abbreviations of the Latin for "of Canterbury", "of York", and "of London"). But Sees that have been created in Protestant times appear to find it difficult to live up to the old Catholic tradition, and so we get "Bradford", "Derby" etc.

The Sees of Peterborough, Gloucester and Chester were created by Henry VIII but have been acknowledged by the Holy See in the Creation of Titular Cathedral Priors since 1633. Such titles, together with those of Titular Abbots, are conferred on members of the English Benedictine Congregation in token of their continuity with the pre-Reformation Abbeys and Priories.

Another title that is popish in its origin is *Fidei Defensor* (Defender of the Faith), which was given to Henry VIII by Pope Leo X in 1521. It is still used in its shortened form, "FID. DEF.", on our coinage.

The Established Church, in the coat of arms used by both the Sees of Canterbury and Armagh, displays the Pallium. The Pallium is given by the Pope when he appoints an archbishop, and he thus invests him with ecclesiastical jurisdiction. Neither of the present Anglican archbishops claims to get his jurisdiction from the Holy See, but the old symbol that once denoted this still lives on.

Pontifex Maximus

Meaning "Supreme Pontiff", this was originally a title of the pagan Chief Priest of Rome. Tertullian used it satirically of the Pope (*De pudicitas* 1.), and it has stuck ever since (*ODCC*), *Oxford Dictionary of Christian Church*. "Pontiff" means "in charge of bridges" and was used of all bishops, not just the Pope.

Curate

The one who has the responsibility for the cure of souls (in a parish) – the parish priest in modern parlance, as opposed to the assistant curate.

The law and university terms

These have Catholic origins. There is the Hilary Term named after St Hilary's Feast day (12th January). This terms begins the day after Plough Monday (q.v.) and ends the Wednesday before Easter. (Hilary was Bishop of Poitiers and died in 368.) The other terms are named Easter, Trinity and Michaelmas. The same titles hold good at the universities to a certain extent.

Chaplain

The keeper of a chapel (q.v.).

Vicar and Rector

Although most people in non-Catholic circles think of all clergy as being "Vicars", in fact the title originally referred to the Rector's representative (*Vicarius sacerdos*), who was given the cure of souls in the absence of the Rector (Latin for "the one who rules"). The majority of absentee Rectors in the later Middle Ages were Abbots, Priors or Masters of Hospices, who were not so much absentees as restricted by the nature of their office. In these situations the Rector would retain the patronage of the living with the right of presentation, but the Vicar was to all intents and purposes the "parish priest". Normally two-thirds of the parish endowments went to the Rector and one-third the Vicar (Canon 32, Fourth Lateran Council, 1215).

After the Reformation, with the sale of Church property, it was possible for a layman to acquire a rectorship, one notable example of this being the lay rectorship of Thurnham in Kent. This is to all intents and purposes a lordship of the manor, with the added responsibility of the upkeep of the chancel of the parish church.

Servus Servorum Dei

This title means "Servant of the Servants of God". It was one of the papal titles adopted by Pope Gregory the Great (590-604).

Archpriest and Archdeacon

The title of Archpriest may now seem obscure, but on the Continent it is still a dignity conferred on a senior canon of a cathedral chapter. Before the Reformation a Bishop would have two assistants to help him in his work: an Archdeacon to supervise in episcopal administration and an Archpriest to deputize at liturgical functions. These posts were both intended to ensure the smooth running of a diocese in the bishop's absence. These two offices were gradually taken over by the title of Vicar-General. However, the title of Archpriest was given to the superior who was appointed by the Pope to govern secular clergy sent to England from seminaries abroad between 1598 and 1621.

Sexton

An English corruption of the title Sacristan, a church official who has charge of the *sacra* ("holy thing"), such as the linen, candles, altar wine, vessels and vestments.

Monsignor

A title given to senior ranks of the clergy, be they Papal Chamberlains, Domestic Prelates (now called papal chaplains) or Proto Notaries Apostolic. These positions at the Papal Court are now defunct, which makes the title a bit of an anachronism.

Canon

Originally this was a title referring to those living under a common rule or Canon. Later two distinct categories of Canon developed: those who were regular (White and Black Canons) and those who were secular, viz. Cathedral Canons or those living a common life not bound by the rule of religious life.

Chancellor

An official in the courts of Roman Canon Law. Originally a Chancellor was simply an usher at the chancel (lattice or screen) separating the public from the court. The title was introduced to England by St Edward the Confessor and implies a secretary of matters relating to Canon Law.

Lord Chancellor

The highest judicial functionary in England, who ranks above all peers except royal princes and the Archbishop of Canterbury. In Catholic times the Lord Chancellor had invariably been a man of the cloth; hence the title, "Keeper of the King's (or Queen's) conscience."

DRESS

The Paris Cap

The biretta is the traditional dress of the University of Milan, but before the Reformation Catholic clergy in England wore the Paris Cap. This was the headgear of the University of Paris, which has since been misnamed the Canterbury Cap. This cap was adopted early on by the Universities of Oxford and Cambridge, but the modern academic cap developed from the need to remove skull–cap and over–cap together (viz. bishops who still wear a skull cap under the biretta) and thus produced a combination of the two.

Almuce

A square-ended hood with a cape, long fur tippets and lined with fur. The clerical rank was indicated by the quality of the fur. Today the Norbertines (White Canons) have a relic of this in the form of a white fur muff over their left arms. The Anglican "scarf" has the same derivation.

Cassock

Before the Reformation secular clergy wore cassocks buttoned from the waist up and tied with a belt. From the waist down they were open and unbuttoned, like the garb of the boys of Christ's Hospital to this day. This was the true Sarum cassock and is distinct from the double-breasted form which is usually so-called. Moreover, it is more than likely that these cassocks were blue in colour. Bishop Richard Challoner's cassock at Allen Hall

Seminary, although of eighteenth-century vintage, retains the Sarum blue colour, with red cuffs, piping and buttons to show his rank. Challoner continued the Sarum tradition, and so this seems reliable evidence.

Purple as the colour for Bishops has only been in vogue since the sixteenth century. The change took place because Pope Pius V (1566-72), being a Dominican, stuck to white. The Cardinals then changed to papal scarlet, and the Bishops adopted the "sacred purple". However, the original colours in each case are retained in the stripe on the cord of the pectoral cross. The papal soutane was granted to English Catholic clergy by Pope Pius IX who, when the English clerics asked what cassock they should wear, declared "Like mine, but black."

Garter robes

King Edward III founded the Order of the Garter to the "honour of the Blessed Virgin". On Our Lady's feasts the knights wore a golden image of Our Lady on the right shoulder of their blue choir mantles (Register of the "Most Noble Order of the Garter", vol. i, p. 48, ed. 1724).

Liturgical colours

Before the Reformation there was a certain latitude regarding liturgical colours. In England there were two colours peculiar to the Sarum use: brick-red vestments for Sundays after Epiphany, and white or buff-coloured vestments with red (symbols of the Passion) for Lent. On Palm Sunday and Good Friday red was the liturgical colour. The only other difference was the yellow vestments worn for Confessors.

The mozzetta

A short cape-like garment to which a small hood is attached; it is worn by the Pope and by Cardinals, Cathedral Canons etc. Military chaplains in the Middle Ages wore *capes de goer* (Norman French for "war capes"); these probably protected the sacraments when the chaplains were going through the lines.

Judges' robes

The ancient connection between the law and the Church is still maintained in many ways. There is, for instance, the custom for judges of the King's Bench to wear certain robes on Saints' days. These robes are really survivals of clerical vestments. The judge's outer robe seems to be a continuation of the cope that was once worn, while the cincture resembles the priest's girdle and the stole is like the ecclesiastical stole. A judge's scarlet ermine-trimmed robe gives way to a purple robe lined with watered silk during the Easter sitting. Such changes of raiment according to the Church's seasons are yet another example of the survival of the ancient Catholic customs. Moreover, the legal wigs still retain the old clerical tonsure.

The cappa nigra

A black cope worn by secular canons in choir before the Reformation.

The cappa parva and the cappa magna

The cappa parva was a violet or scarlet hood with a long cape worn by prelates and cardinals in late mediaeval times. The cappa magna was a very lengthy version of the same thing, needing a train-bearer.

Academic robes

The academic dress of Oxford and Cambridge is derived from pre-Reformation clerical dress. For example, the red gown of the Oxford DD was once in the form of a red cassock, which was how the cleric manifested his academic status. A diaphanous alb or rochet ensured that the colour was still seen. This desire to be recognized by colour continued with the introduction of lace in post-Reformation times. The present academic hood is now a useless piece of ornament, which was expanded in the eighteenth century to accommodate full-bottomed wigs. The original pre-Reformation hood was in the "liripipe" shape and could actually be put to use as a hood.

Clerical neckwear

The clerical cassock has mediaeval origins, and the shirt as originally worn under the cassock was the same as any other mediaeval shirt – that is, it was gathered into pleats and tied at the neck by a cord laced through a standing collar, which opened at the back or the front (cf. the amice still worn by the celebrant at Mass). As fashion developed shirts displayed a folded collar, which for the cleric simply folded over the top of his cassock, a fashion still beloved of the Oratorians. From the elongated shapes of these collars the "preaching bands" developed. It is interesting to note how they have survived in the legal profession as a reminder that some courts were originally ecclesiastical. In France black bands with white borders were introduced for walking out and evening dress.

In England in Penal times (when Catholicism was outlawed) clerical dress had disappeared, although when the community which today makes up the Abbey of Downside first settled in the West Country it was outstanding for its blue frock-coats and white stocks (cravats), a dress not unsimilar to the court dress of the day. Interestingly enough, George V changed court dress to a winged collar with a white bow tie. This is still the official dress of the Anglican clergy, and the tradition (at least so far as the white bow tie is concerned) is still kept up at Oxford and Cambridge, where membership once implied clerical status. Catholic clergy, on the other hand, have adopted (as many others have since) the "Roman Collar", which is presumed to have been introduced to England by the Rosminians in 1835.

The clerical beard

By tradition hermits have always worn beards, hence they are worn by members of the Carthusian and Camaldolese orders. In the early days of Christianity the beard became firmly established among all clergy, and in the East it has remained

unchallenged to this day. The shaven chin eventually became a characteristic of Latin Christianity, although during the sixteenth century beards became so fashionable that many clerics adopted them and thus provoked a controversy on the propriety of the clerical beard (Caesar Baronius wrote a treatise on the subject).

However, beards went out of fashion in the late seventeenth century and did not become fashionable again until the nineteenth, by which time they were considered to be on the whole incorrect for priests. Missionaries could always claim exemption from being clean shaven, and a bearded tradition has persisted unaccountably in France. But to this day those visiting the Holy Land for any length of time would be expected to grow a beard out of sympathy with a tradition that goes back to the Apostles.

In all this the Capuchins remain somewhat distinct, as their founder, Matteo di Bassi, intended a return to the simple eremitical life of the early Franciscans and promoted beards. However, the beard's association with the hermit's life was soon forgotten.

CUSTOMS

Spilling salt

This was held to be unlucky (it was thought that the person had been jogged by the Devil), hence salt was thrown over the left shoulder with the right hand (to put salt on the tail (q.v.) of the Devil). In Leonardo da Vinci's *Last Supper* Judas is shown spilling the salt. Salt was used in Baptism to symbolically cast out evil. It is an emblem of purity, and hence it has been put in coffins to ward off the Devil.

Simnel cakes

Originally these were eaten on Midient Sunday (Laetare Sunday), a time of relaxation from the Lenten rigours. They were also eaten at Easter and Christmas. The word "simnel" is derived from the old French and Latin *simila* (a word for the finest wheat flour).

The Wedding Breakfast

According to Catholic custom, marriage took place at a Nuptial Mass, and both bride and bridgegroom received Holy Communion. As they would both have been fasting, according to the Church's law for those who communicate, they needed their breakfast after the ceremony. Their friends would join them at the meal, and hence the origin of the "Wedding Breakfast".

When, at the Reformation, both the Nuptial Mass and the law of fasting before Communion ceased, the breakfast following the ceremony lost its meaning. But the custom has carried on in name until the present time, and, of course, it remained of practical importance to Catholics until the fasting laws were changed in 1953.

The holy number thirteen

An interesting survival of Catholic days is the religious significance attached to the number thirteen, in spite of the efforts of the Reformers to stamp out the tradition by calling the number unlucky. The model in men's minds from quite early times seems to have been Our Divine Lord and the twelve Apostles, and this number of thirteen was copied in all kinds of ways. For example, if a benefactor wanted to found some almshouses (or a hospital, as almshouses were often called), as a rule, thirteen of them would be built. Thus Hugh II, Abbot of Reading, founded a hospital for thirteen poor men and thirteen poor women, about the year 1190. The Herald's College in London which was founded by Richard III had (and still has) thirteen members. Catherine of Braganza, wife of Charles II, brought a body of Portuguese Franciscans to London in 1662, the community consisting of a Father Guardian and twelve friars. A "baker's dozen" consisted of thirteen loaves or cakes, and there was legislation connected with this custom.

But an interesting survival of thirteen being regarded as a lucky number is to be found in the common custom of putting a hen to sit on thirteen eggs. When a sitting of eggs is advertised for sale, the number is always understood to be thirteen. If this number is really unlucky, as has been made out in modern times, are the thirteen eggs put under the hen a bad omen? Surely this is for good luck. The interesting thing about this old custom, with its religious tinge, is that it should have come down to us intact all the long way from our Catholic past. And it shows also how deeply matters connected with religion, in however small a way, entered into the daily life of our forefathers.

The "Devil's door"

Traditionally the prayer of exorcism was prayed before the sacrament of Baptism was given; this was to dispel any spirit hostile to God. For this reason fonts were always placed opposite the north door of a church, which would be left ajar during the exorcism prayer in order to let the Devil escape – hence the "Devil's door". (*DS*)

The Devil's side of the churchyard

There was a tradition that good Christians were only buried on the south and east sides of the churchyard. Those who had suffered capital punishment or had taken their own lives were buried on the north side, by the "Devil's door" (q.v.). (*DS*)

Parvis

This is a low Latin corruption of *paradisus* to produce "parvisus". Originally the word "parvis" referred to a church close. Later the word meant the place or court before the main entrance of a cathedral. In the parvis of St Paul's, London, lawyers used to meet for consultation. The word is applied today to the room above the church porch (cf. Rycote, Oxon.).

> *A sergeant of lawe, war and wys,*
> *That often hadde ben atte parvys.*
> Chaucer, *Canterbury Tales* (*BDPF*)

The kiss of peace

This is part of the liturgy of the Mass but is omitted on Maundy Thursday to avoid imitation of Judas, who betrayed Our Lord with a "kiss" on that day. In mediaeval times a "pax brede" was used; this was a representation of the crucifixion or some such scene on a flat object with a handle, and this was passed around for everyone to kiss. Normally the kiss of peace was given before Communion, in accordance with the verse, "first make peace with your brother, and then offer your gift at the altar" (Matthew 5:24). The bridal kiss in the Nuptial Mass took place before Communion according to the old Sarum rubric (*Missa*

Sponsalium). Today the kiss of peace is called the sign of peace and is more often a handshake.

The Court of Peculiars

A branch of the Court of Arches (q.v.) which had jurisdiction over "peculiars" – i.e. those churches which were exempt from episcopal jurisdiction (religious and royal chapels).

Chantry

An endowed chapel where daily Mass was offered for the souls of those specified. This word also means the endowment for the saying of such Masses. The chantries were abolished unlawfully at the Reformation, but they continue in some ancient family chapels (cf. Fitzalan Chapel, Arundel).

Chapel

This word originally meant a chest containing relics, or a shrine that housed them. The word derives from *capella* ("little cloak"), which was the name given to the piece of cloak which St Martin of Tours had cut off from his own to protect a freezing beggar. This *capella* was kept as a sacred relic by the Frankish Kings, and the place where it was housed was called a *chapelle* and the keeper a *chapelain*. Thus the name came to be attached to a small or private place of worship. The term "printing chapel" (an association of compositors and machine men) is said to derive from when printing was first set up in chapels attached to religious houses, such as Caxton's press at Westminster Abbey.

The elder tree

A tree of evil association, for according to popular legend it was the tree on which Judas hanged himself. Sir John Manderville (c. 1364), speaking of the well of Siloam, wrote: "Fast by is the elder tree on which Judas hanged himself." Shakespeare wrote: "Judas was hanged on an elder" (*Love's Labour's Lost* V.ii). It was a tree to be avoided.

Ember days

The Wednesdays, Fridays and Saturdays of the four Ember weeks. These were fixed by the Council of Placentia (1095) as those weeks containing the first Sunday in Lent, Whit Sunday, Holy Cross Day and St Lucy's Day. The Ember days were days of special prayer and fasting. The word derives from the Middle English "ymber" (a "circuit").

The Red Cross

The Red Cross was first adopted for his hospitaller brothers by St Camillus of Lellis in 1591. St Camillus established the first military ambulance unit. It was in action at the Battle of Solferino in 1591, when his brethren drove horse-drawn wagons, with the Red Cross clearly displayed on both sides, through the battle lines to care for the sick and wounded. The Red Cross was intended not as a heraldic symbol but as an indication of neutrality. Henry Dunan, the founder of the modern international organization known as the Red Cross, took the emblem directly from St Camillus. He shortened the Latin cross, thus producing the Greek-type cross now so familiar to us.

Palmer

A pilgrim to the Holy Land who was privileged to carry a palm staff, and who spent all his days visiting shrines and living on charity.

> *The faded palm-branch in his hand*
> *Showed pilgrim from the Holy Land.*
>
> Scott, *Marimon* I:27

The Cross of St John (or the Maltese Cross)

This is the cross borne by the Catholic Hospitaller Order of St John of Jerusalem, Rhodes and Malta. In shape it is like four barbed arrowheads joined at the points. Because of its eight points it is also known as the Cross of the Beatitudes. Like the Red Cross, the Cross of St John has been adopted by many other organizations.

The Fisherman's Ring

A seal ring with which each Pope is invested at his election. It is used only for sealing papal briefs. It is officially broken at the death of a Pope by the Chamberlain of the Pontifical Household. Its device is that of St Peter fishing from a boat.

Shaveling

When priests and religious men wore the tonsure (still seen in some countries today), secular clergy had a small shaven patch

on the back of their heads, while the religious had a much larger area. "Shaveling" was a term of derision used against the clergy. John Bradford (1510–55), a Marian Martyr, wrote: "It maketh no matter how thou live here, so thou have the favour of the Pope and his shavelings." (*BDPF*)

Doles

The origin of doles in England is connected with funerals. After a Requiem Mass a feast was shared. This was to soften grief for widows and orphans and to make food available to the needy. More often than not the deceased willed the distribution of a dole, which also provided for those who assisted in the obsequies. These doles were sometimes in the form of money or clothing.

A London mercer named Symonds left instructions in his will (1586) for the distribution of penny loaves to twelve poor persons chosen by the Lord Mayor; the loaves were to be placed beneath Symonds' picture in St Paul's. On one Sunday in each quarter the dean or the bishop were to decide who got the loaves.

Perhaps the most historic dole is that of Tichborne in Hampshire. In the reign of Henry II, Sir Roger de Tichborne's wife Dame Mabella, who was sick and bedridden, petitioned her husband to establish a dole of bread at Tichborne for all poor persons who might ask for it on each succeeding Feast of the Annunciation. Sir Roger, to support the annual dole, promised as much land within the vicinity of his estate as his ailing wife could cover while a brand continued to burn. To his surprise, his invalid wife crawled around twenty-six acres. She was conveyed back to bed, where she pronounced a malediction on any who would discontinue the dole – if they did so, the result would be the failure of the male line of the Tichbornes. Prosperity would

attend the family as long as the dole continued. It is interesting to note that during the last war an annual dole was missed, and the male line subsequently ended. However, the dole continues today.

The Hospital of St Cross at Winchester has traditionally always given a dole of bread and ale (a "wayfarer dole") to passing travellers. This is in fact the sole surviving dole of its kind dating from pre-Reformation times. (Cf. William Andrews, FRHS, *Curiosities of the Church*, London, 1890.)

Curfew

Curfew in England, it has been said, was first introduced under Norman rule. At eight in the evening a bell was rung to indicate that everyone had to put out or cover their fires and extinguish all their lights. This was supposedly introduced under William the Conqueror to prevent conspiracies among the turbulent Saxons. But in fact the curfew bell was tolled throughout Europe long before the Norman Conquest. This was simply a practical precaution; most dwellings were made of wood, wattle and straw, so the curfew was a measure to reduce the danger of conflagration. Indeed, by King Alfred's time it was a well-established custom. He ordained that a bell be rung at eight o'clock each evening in the university town of Oxford and that all fires be covered at the signal.

The word "curfew" is derived from the old French *couvre-feu*, which meant literally "cover fire". Moreover, there was a household object known as a *couvre-fer*, a kind of solid metal fire-guard. The intention was not so much to put out fires but to cover them and damp them down for the night, thus ensuring continued warmth.

The curfew did become rigorously enforced under Norman rule. Tradition has it that as the Conqueror lay dying the curfew bell tolled, and he asked for prayers for his soul. This may be coincidental with the Catholic custom of saying the *de Profundis* for the departed at the hour of curfew. The fifteenth Duke of Norfolk certainly had the *de Profundis* said for his first wife (the Duchess Flora) at this hour. The bell tolled five times, then three times, then twice and then once. Although Henry I is supposed to have abolished the obligation of curfew, the custom continued. Indeed, the office of parish clerk of St Mary-le-Bow was specifically for the ringing of curfew. Today the custom has largely ceased and is perhaps only associated with Grey's elegy, "The curfew tolls the knell of parting day".

Lich-gate

The covered entrance to a churchyard intended to provide shelter for the coffin and the mourners while they awaited the officiating priest ("lic" was the Anglo-Saxon word for "body").

St Boniface's Cup

An extra cup of wine. Pope Boniface XI instituted an indulgence to those who drank his health (or the health of the reigning Pontiff) after grace – *Ebrietatis Einconium*. He was elected by the mob in 896 and reigned for only fifteen days, having twice been unflocked. His election was uncanonical.

Evensong

The old English word for parish Vespers and Compline as sung in churches before the Reformation.

Touching for the "King's Evil"

William of Malmesbury in his work *King of England* (1066) describes how a young woman developed swollen glands and became much disfigured. She dreamt that a cure was wrought by the King's touch, and so, upon waking, she went to his palace, whereupon the King "rubbed the woman's neck with his fingers dipped in water: a speedy recovery followed his healing hands". The King in question was Edward the Confessor, who was described by Polydore Vergil (*English History* Vol. VIII, 1534) as "onlie touchings, bie the divine power of Godde, to heale the swellinge in the throat . . . termed the King's evil".

The tradition of "touching" continued with the Stuart Kings

of England down to the time of James II. William III dismissed the custom; since he was not of the direct line he was not considered to have the gift. One of the last persons to be "touched" in England was Dr Johnson: in 1712, when he was less than three years old he was "touched" by Queen Anne. Henry VII began the custom of giving a small gold or silver coin to the person "touched", called a touchpiece (some of these are on view in the Castle Museum at Chidingstone). Charles II "touched" 92,107 persons *in toto*; some were actually crushed in the rush (Macaulay, *History of England*, chap. 14).

Bowing to the Speaker

When a Member of Parliament rises to speak in the House he bows in the direction of the Speaker. This is not out of respect for that office. Parliament first met in the Chapel of St Stephen in Westminster Palace, and the practice of bowing in the direction of the altar continues.

The right of sanctuary

Sanctuary, by tradition, was a refuge for anyone who had broken the law or who had politically miscalculated and wished to escape retribution. In England a code of law was drawn up in 693 by Ina, King of the West Saxons, which specifically recognized the rights of sanctuary. The code stipulated that if he took refuge in a church, even someone accused of a capital offence escaped the death penalty; however, he had to make compensation for his crime. King Alfred in 887 introduced laws to allow those fleeing justice (slight offences only) to spend three nights in a church in safety. Alfred had such fugitives protected by the force of the

law, and heavy fines were exacted upon those who infringed the rights of sanctuary.

William the Conqueror added to the laws of sanctuary in 1070. The rights of sanctuary were to be temporary – forty days in all, during which time the fugitive could come to terms with his pursuers. If this failed he had to appear before the coroner's court clothed in sackcloth, confess his crime and quit the realm (sacrilege and high treason obviated any rights of sanctuary).

In 1529 Henry VIII's legislation directed that after the confession the fugitive had to be branded with the letter "A" on his right arm, indicating that he had abjured the realm. If the offender failed after forty days to confess his crime before the coroner and remained in sanctuary, anyone assisting him was considered guilty of a felony.

Abjuration of the realm was followed by a swift escort by the parish constable to a suitable port. Many sanctuary men who reached the port of Dover in fact escaped to the forests of the Kentish Weald to join an ever-increasing band of outlaws. On the other hand, those who reached foreign lands would vouchsafe national secrets or teach foreigners the English longbow. This suspected breach of national security resulted in the sanctuary men being confined in a suitable place within the realm. To leave confinement without royal pardon brought the threat of trial for the original or supposed crime, without the protection of sanctuary. Sanctuary people had to wear a badge to indicate their status and could not carry a sword or stay away from their sanctuary overnight.

Henry VIII endeavoured to reduce the rights of sanctuary in 1540. Only parish churches and churchyards, cathedrals, hospitals and the special sanctuaries of Westminster, Wells, Manchester, Northampton, Norwich, York, Derby and Launceston could claim the right. Those claiming sanctuary in Manchester had become so numerous that the privilege was suspended and given to Chester instead. The statutes of 1540 also excluded sanctuary for wilful murder, rape, burglary, highway robbery and arson, and no more than twenty persons were to be sheltered at a sanctuary at any one time.

In 1624 James I's legislation abolished most aspects of the sanctuary system. However, for debtors sanctuary continued in a modified form until 1697, when William III's Parliament passed an act to abolish this.

In certain sanctuaries it was necessary to touch an object in order to obtain the benefits. At Durham and Arundel fugitives had to grasp a door-knocker, while at Beverley and Flexham they had to sit upon the "frith stool" or "chair of peace". Although sanctuary as an eccliastical refuge was formally abolished in 1697, other aspects lingered on for civil processes until 1723. (Cf. William Andrews, *Old Church Lore*, London 1891.)

Saluting Our Lady

At Winchester, Wykehamist scholars once doffed their hats in respect to the statue of Our Lady, the Christ Child, the Archangel Gabriel and William of Wykeham, before entering Middle Gate. Commoners did not. Today the custom continues despite the empty niche, where once stood Our Lady.

Benefit of clergy

This was originally the exemption from trial by a secular court of anyone in holy orders or minor orders. It was abolished in 1827 by George IV.

Sudarion

The sweat-cloth used by bishops and abbots to protect their croziers from clammy hands.

Care cloth

A silk or linen cloth formerly laid over newly married couples or held over them as a canopy.

Houseling cloth

A strip of linen held across the chancel to catch any fallen pieces of the Sacrament at Holy Communion. It has been used since mediaeval times and was still in use up to the Second Vatican Council (1963–65).

"Touch wood"

This is a saying which has remained popular. It originated, of course, from the touching of the wood of the true Cross, the

most prized relic. Many a Catholic would venerate such a relic before beginning a hazardous task. Today most people are satisfied with touching any wood as a substitute. By tradition the wood of the Cross was from the aspen tree, which is why the aspen always trembles. (*DS*)

Walking under ladders

Like the number thirteen, this was considered a good omen until the Puritans associated it with bad luck. The ladder was a symbol of Our Lord's Passion, and therefore to walk under it was a sign of redemption in that it inclined to the Cross from where Christ's blood flowed for mankind. It is also related that a ladder against a wall, since it forms a triangle, represents the Holy Trinity, and that to go under it is therefore a good omen.

Altar rails

These were not a Catholic custom – the screen and moveable kneeling-desks were the standard Catholic furnishings. The Anglican Bishop Wren (uncle of Sir Christopher) ordered a "rayle" which was "so thick with pillars that doggs may not gett in" (*Daily Telegraph* 5.3.62).

Church bells

Another place where we can find traces of the old religion is in the inscriptions that were often made on the outsides of church bells. We find saints' names in great numbers, such as St Thomas, St Clement, St Augustine, St Ann, St Margaret and St Catherine, followed by the usual prayer, "Pray for us." Inscriptions in honour of Our Lady run through endless forms, such as "O pious Jesu, Mary's Flower", or "Thou, O Christ, wilt protect us through the prayers of Thy Mother", or "Pray with pious mind for us, O Virgin Mary". There are countless inscriptions of this kind up in our old church towers, and the bells are telling of the old faith every time they are rung. In the Middle Ages they were rung at times of tempest or thunderstorm to drive away evil spirits (Caxton's *Golden Legend*, 1483).

The Marybell (or *the pardon bell*)

(Three rings of three and a ring of nine) A name given to the Angelus bell rung at dawn, noon and dusk, when the Angelus was recited. (The morning and evening Angles were established by Archbishop Arundel's mandate of 1399: see Appendix "Dowry of Mary".) It was also called the pardon bell because of the indulgence attached to certain prayers said in the Angelus.

The de Profundis bell

Five slow single rings for verses and versicle, and three, two and one short rings for collect. This was usually rung at seven or eight o'clock in the evening (cf. curfew, q.v.), when the psalm, *de Profundis* was said for the departed.

The passing bell

The passing bell was so called because it was rung when a person was near death or at the time of burial; the bell was intended to invoke the prayers of all who heard it. St Bede gives one of the earliest references to this custom, when describing the obsequies of St Hilda. In 1526 the churchwarden of the parish of Holchurch recorded in his accounts:

> Item. The clerke to have for tollynge of the passynge belle for manne, womanne or childes, if it be the day – 4d.
> Item. If it be in the night, for the same – 8d.

In Shakespeare's *Henry IV Part Two* we read:

> *And his tongue*
> *Sounds ever after as a sullen bell*
> *Remembered knolling a departing friend.*

The tolling of the passing bell continued until the reign of Charles II. To this day some churches still ring a bell to denote a funeral. So the old adage still holds good: "When the bell begins to toll, Lord have mercy on the soul."

The sacring bell (or the sanctus bell)

The bell rung at the consecration and at the elevation in the Mass. The name comes from the word *sanctus*, which heralds the consecration. "He heard a little sacring bell ring to the elevation of a tomorrow Mass" (Reginald Scott, *Discovery of Witchcraft*, 1584). (*BDPF*)

Good luck and horseshoes

One day when St Dunstan was engaged in his smithy at Mayfield the Devil made one of his regular visits. Dunstan, being particularly incensed by this unwelcome intrusion, seized the Devil by the nose with his red-hot tongs. On another occasion the Devil appeared as a traveller asking to have his horse shod, but Dunstan recognized him and set about him. So severely did

the Archbishop beat him that in his extremity the Devil begged for mercy. Dunstan thereupon made him promise not to enter any house where a horseshoe was hung. Hence good luck is associated with horseshoes.

The Feast of the Ass

This feast was more properly kept at the Cathedral of Beauvais in France. It commemorated the ass upon which the Holy Family took flight into Egypt. The celebrations took place on 14th January. A young girl with a child in her arms, representing the Blessed Virgin and the baby Jesus, rode up to the high altar on an ass singing "the song of the Ass". There is no similar tradition in England, but there was an unofficial tradition which became more of a folk custom than a Church ceremony. These folk customs which celebrated midwinter or midsummer often became a little confused, and this probably accounts for the features of the celebrated ass in Shakespeare's *A Midsummer Night's Dream*.

Peter Pence

An annual tribute of one penny paid to Rome on the feast of St Peter. Originally it was paid by every family, but later only by those who had at least thirty pence's worth of stock. The paying of Peter Pence in Britain appears to have been started by Offa II, King of Mercia; at that time it was called "Romescot". After St Augustine's mission the English developed a great devotion to St Peter, but it was King Alfred the Great who made Peter Pence an official collection to support the Roman Pontiff. The tribute was abolished by Henry VIII in 1534, but revived by the Catholic hierarchy in the nineteenth century. It is now collected on the Sunday closest to the Feast of St Peter and St Paul (29th June).

Church Scot

A tribute paid on St Martin's Day (11th November) in support of the clergy in Anglo-Saxon times. The Anglo-Saxon word "sceat" (the name of a coin) gave rise to "scot".

St Christopher's image

In many mediaeval churches there was a large wall painting of St Christopher opposite the main door. It was a common belief that all who looked upon his image would suffer no harm that day (he was the patron saint of travellers). According to legend he was a giant who carried the Christ-child over a river. His name comes from the Greek *Christopheron* and means "Christ-bearer".

Blessing those who sneeze

During the time of the early Church a plague broke out in Rome whose first symptom was a sneeze. A pious Christian would thus

bless anyone who sneezed (Caxton's *Golden Legend*, 1483). The Great Plague of London had a similar symptom – hence the nursery rhyme, "Ring of Roses" goes, "Atishoo, atishoo, we all fall down!" (*DS*)

The Ecclesia Anglicana

The name for the Catholic Church of England which was used by the papacy in its diplomatic correspondence. Since the Reformation this title has been "poached" by the Anglicans.

"Remember," said King Charles

King Charles I's last word on the scaffold, said to Bishop Juxon. This has been interpreted in terms of King Charles' belief that he was suffering as a result of his failure to return the property which had been seized from the Catholic Church by Henry VIII. It is said that he was a Catholic at heart, and saw his sufferings as a divine visitation. He had therefore made a vow that if he survived his imprisonment, the property of the Church would be returned. His word to Juxon was intended to encourage his son to fulfil the vow. (*BDPF*)

MISCELLANEOUS

St Peter's haddock

According to tradition it was in the mouth of a haddock that St Peter found the coin in Matthew 17:27, and the two marks on the fish's neck are said to be the impressions of Peter's finger and thumb.

> O superstitious dainty, Peter's fish,
> How com'st thou here to make so godly a dish.
>
> Metallus, *Dialogues*, 1693

Lambeth Degrees

By the Peter Pence Act of 1533 Archbishops of Canterbury (then in communion with Rome) could grant degrees. Under a different authority this custom continues today.

Our Lord's donkey

On the back of a donkey the fur makes the shape of a cross. It is said that this commemorates the occasion when Our Lord made His triumphal entry into Jerusalem on a donkey.

"Telling one's beads"

In Old English a "bead" was a prayer, and as prayers were "told" the saying, "telling one's beads" arose. This applied particularly

97

to the "paternoster" (ten "Our Father" beads and one "glory be") and, in the sixteenth century, to the Rosary. The original bidding prayers at Mass were called the "Bidding of Beads".

"Cooing and billing"

This expression originally described Queen Mary and her husband King Philip of Spain as portrayed on a 1555 shilling. This showed them face to face rather than side by side. Hence the verse:

> Still amorous, and fond, and billing,
> Like Philip and Mary on a shilling.
> Hudibras Part III.1, S. Butler (1612–80)

"Old Nick"

A corruption of the name of Niccolo Machiavelli, who wrote *The Prince* in the sixteenth century as a guide to statecraft. So cunning and cynical was the advice which he gave to princes that his nickname was applied to the Devil.

> Nick Machiavelli had ne'er a trick
> (Though he gives his name to our Old Nick).
> Hudibras Part III.1

Dunce

This word derives from the name of Duns Scotus (c. 1265–1308), a Franciscan friar and famous mediaeval schoolman who was born at Dunse in Scotland. His opponents called his followers "Dunces".

The Judicium Crucis

A form of ordeal in which two opponents stretched out their arms before a cross, until one of them could hold out no longer and lost his cause. It is said that a Bishop of Paris and an Abbot of St Denis appealed to this form of judgement in dispute. (*BDPF*)

The Bain Marie

The French name for a double saucepan. The Latin name was *Balneum Mariae* (Mrs Glasse's *Cookery Book*, 1796), and in Ben Johnson's *Alchemist* (II.iii) it is called "St Mary's bath". It is thought that these names refer to the gentleness of this method of heating. (*BDPF*)

Legem pone

Old slang for money paid down on the nail; ready money (pone). The words were taken from the beginning of Pslam 119: *Legem pone mihi, Domine, viam justificationum tuarum* ("Teach me, O Lord, the way of thy statutes"). This was the psalm which used to be read on the morning of the twenty-fifth day of each month.

> Use legem pone to pay at thy day,
> But use not ovemus for often delay.
>
> Tusser, Good Husbandry, 1557

Paludament

A distinctive mantle worn by Roman generals. This was the "scarlet robe" given to Our Lord at His mockery and trial (Matthew 27:28). (*BDPF*)

Kissing the Pope's toe

Matthew of Westminster relates that it was once the custom to kiss the papal toe. This practice was said to have originated in the eighth century when a comely woman not only kissed the Pope's hand but also gave it an affectionate squeeze. The susceptible old Pontiff, realizing the danger of carnal desire, afterwards only proffered his foot. The papal slippers were in fact embroidered with crosses, to indicate where they should be kissed. One mischievous early mediaeval papal legate, dealing with some particularly unruly royal delegates, wore steel sabots, and at the opportune moment delivered a sharp kick in the teeth! The custom of kissing the Pope's toe has now been superseded by a genuflection and a kiss on the papal ring.

St Pancras

One of the patron saints of children (cf. St Nicholas). He was martyred in the Diocletian persecution (304) at Rome at the age of thirteen. The first church to be consecrated in England by St Augustine of Canterbury was dedicated to St Pancras.

Santa Claus

A contraction of Santa Nikolaus (St Nicholas), patron of Germany, where presents were given on his feast (6th December). He is also one of the patron saints of children.

Basilica

This is taken from the Greek *basilikos*, meaning "royal". The Imperial courts of justice in Rome had a nave, aisles and an apse, where the Emperor's throne was situated. These courts were adapted to worship by the early Christians after Constantine had made them over to the Church.

Religious plays

The theatre began in the Church and priests were the first actors. To this day the ceremonies of Holy Week – Palm Sunday processions, Maundy Thursday foot washing and the Stations of the Cross – are all dramatic presentations of Our Lord's Passion and the clergy are still the principal actors.

There were three types of religious drama in mediaeval England: mystery plays, miracle plays and morality plays. The authors were intent on showing the fulfilment of the Old Testament in the New and the salvation of mankind through

Christ's Nativity, Passion and Resurrection. Biblical events were covered by the mystery plays, the lives of the saints were the subject of the miracle plays and in the morality plays allegory was used to teach religious truths. The first recorded miracle play was *The Miracle of St Catharine*, performed at Dunstable in 1110. A number of plays by a monk named Hilarius have survived including *The Image of St Nicholas*, *The Raising of Lazarus* and the story of *Daniel*.

Initially the priests took the principal parts, but eventually the laity took over and local church guilds became responsible for the performances. Originally the performances took place in church, then in churchyards and subsequently in public thoroughfares. The stage would be constructed on wheels on three levels representing Heaven, Earth and Hell. Hell was represented by a whale's open jaws, behind which a fire was lit. This is well depicted by a fresco on the chancel arch in the Chapel of the Holy Cross, Stratford-upon-Avon.

Four sets of ancient plays are still extant: they are known as the Chester, Wakefield, Coventry and York series. A monk named Ralph Higden (d. 1363) wrote a series of twenty-five plays which were performed by the Chester Trade Guilds on Monday, Tuesday and Wednesday in Whitsun week. *Noah's Flood* was a very popular mystery play and has enjoyed a recent revival. The play opens with the entrance of God, who, after lamenting the world's wickedness, decides to unleash the Flood. Noah appears and constructs the ark. When the ark is finished God hands Noah an inventory of all the animals he is to take on board. All the animals and people enter the ark, with the exception of Noah's wife – she refuses to board unless she can bring her gossipy friends. Mrs Noah is finally compelled to enter and proceeds to box Noah's ears. Noah complains about the nature of womankind. In the end all are safely delivered.

Bishop Bonner in 1542 issued a proclamation forbidding the acting of clergy and the presentation of plays in church in his Diocese of London. However, all was not lost, for though religious plays did end at the Reformation, secular drama subsequently became well established in the country. Recently there has been a small revival of religious plays as part of a rediscovery of local Christian culture. (Cf. William Andrews, *Curiosities of the Church*, London, 1890.)

103

Weeping crosses

Weeping crosses were places where people went to repent of their misdeeds. There were such crosses at Oxford, Shrewsbury and Stafford. "The tyme will come when comming home by weeping crosse, thou shalt confesse that it is better to be at home in the care of a hermit than abroad in the court of an Emperor" (*Euphues and his England* 1580, by John Lyly).

Roman purple

Roman purple originated in the Phoenician city of Tyre. The dye was obtained from shellfish. Alexander the Great, when seizing the treasures of Darius of Persia, found a large quantity of Tyrian purple. This colour came to be associated in particular with Imperial Rome. It seems that the Levant was not alone in supplying this colour, for in Acts 16:14 we read of a certain Lydia from Thyatira who was in the purple dye trade. For fifteen hundred years Tyrian purple was famous in the ancient world, but manufacture ceased at about the time of the Emperor Justinian (the sixth century) – the shellfish, no doubt, were over-fished. A whelk-like mollusc, called Purpura produced a dark purple dye and a shellfish called Murex made a lighter one; it was the mixture of these two that produced the famous Tyrian purple.

The Emperor Constantine, upon leaving Rome for his new capital, bestowed on Pope Sylvester the trappings of the Roman court, including the Imperial purple (see p. xxx). The various ranks of prelate (Monsignors, Protonotaries Apostolic etc.) are still distinguished by violet, crimson and true purple, or the shade that goes back to the traditions of the ancient Tyrian people.

A rich purple dye was also made at Meliboea in Thessaly. The *ostrum* fish was used in its manufacture.

> *A military vest of purple flowed,*
> *Lovelier than Meliboean.*
> Milton, *Paradise Lost*, 11:242.

Roman scarlet

This colour was originally exclusive to the Roman Pontiff, but when Pius V in the sixteenth century opted to retain the white robes of his Dominican order, the College of Cardinals who had always been clothed in sacred purple, made a successful plea to adopt the abandoned scarlet (the Pope however retains the use of scarlet hat, cape and shoes). For generations the same family in the city of Cologne made it their business to dye cassocks in the authentic Roman scarlet for the Sacred College. What has become of this practice today is a matter of some speculation (Sacheverell Sitwell, *Truffle Hunt*, London, 1953, p. 81).

Snuff and the Vatican

In the 1950s a snuff-mill near Barcelona still supplied snuff to the Vatican. This was of a particularly percussive nature, and probably as a result Pius IX forbade the offering of snuff on the altar. Snuff could, however, be taken up to the "Gloria in Excelsis". St Philip Neri was a prodigious snuff-taker. When his body was exhumed for the process of canonization, it was found that his nose had suffered total corruption. Despite this being a possible obstacle to canonization he was still raised to the altars of the Church, allowing all to accept that snuff-taking was no bar to sainthood. (Barcelona snuff-mill, cf. Sacheverell Sitwell, *Truffle Hunt*, London, 1953.)

The Placebo

Placebo is the Latin for "I shall please". It was taken from Psalm 116:9, which was used in vespers of the dead. The first antiphon began *Placebo Domini in regione vivorum* ("I shall please [or "walk before"] the Lord in the land of the living"). Those wishing to get rich by ingraciating themselves with the heir to the deceased would sing the "Placebo". This came to mean

> *Flatereres been the develes chapelleyus mere flattery*
> *That singen evere Placebo.*
>
> Chaucer, *Parson's Tale*, XL

Papal Zouaves

A corps of Zouaves (light infantry) was raised in Quebec in 1868 and travelled to Rome to defend the Pope against Garibaldi. They arrived too late, returned to Canada and continued as a regiment. The Holy Father, out of gratitude for their somewhat belated defence of his person, allowed them to eat meat on Fridays for the rest of their lives. (Sacheverell Sitwell, *Truffle Hunt*, London, 1953.)

St Bernard's soup

According to a sixteenth-century tradition, a beggar once asked for bread at a great house and was given a stone. He asked if he might have some boiled water to turn the stone into soup, and then he asked for vegetables and seasoning. Finally he asked the servants to taste the soup, which they pronounced excellent. St Bernard's name was probably added to give authenticity.

The Black Parliament

The name given to the Parliament that opened in November 1529 for the purpose of furthering Henry VIII's seizure of Church property. During six years this Parliament carried out the unlawful sequestration of lands and religious houses without hesitation. (*BDPF*)

The Black Rood of Scotland

A piece of the true Cross set in an ebony crucifix, which St Margaret, wife of King Malcolm Canmore, left to Scotland in 1093. It fell into English hands at the Battle of Neville's Cross in 1346 and was deposited in St Cuthbert's shrine at Durham. It has been lost since the Reformation.

Anno Domini

A term coined by St Bede to designate the years after the birth of Christ.

The Gregorian calendar

Britain changed from the Julian calendar (named after Julius Caesar) to the Gregorian calendar (named after Pope Gregory

XIII) in 1752. This had the effect of adding eleven days to the date. When the Gregorian calendar began in 1582 dates were written with the words, *Stilo Novo*.

> *And so I leave you to your stilo novo.*
> Beaumont and Fletcher, *Woman's Prize*, IV.4

Leap Year

The statistical curiosity of the leap year occurs (usually) every four years, when the earth does not go round the sun in a neat 365 days, but 365 days, 5 hours, 48 minutes and 45.9747 seconds. The solution proposed by Sosigenes in AD 150 was to make the leap year 366 days. This was revised by the Emperor Augustus and Pope Gregory XIII in 1582, to create the modern calendar. The custom of women proposing in a leap year is said to date back to St Patrick, who, after a riot in a nunnery, agreed to allow girls to pop the question. (*The Times*, 29th February 1992)

The pawnbrokers' sign

The pawnbrokers' three golden balls are said to have originated from the Lombardian bankers (cf. Lombard Street, London), such as the Medici. But the Medici arms contain five red balls and one blue ball with three *fleurs de lys*. However, the pawnbrokers' sign may have been based on the symbol of St Nicholas of Bari, which was three bags of gold. He was said to have given a bag of gold each to three sisters to enable them to have marriage dowries.

TRADITIONS AT SEA

Saluting the quarterdeck

This is in fact an old religious custom. Our sailors still salute the quarterdeck; all ranks are strictly obliged to do so. The salute is given to the place where a crucifix always hung in Catholic days.

No launching on a Friday

A ship is never launched on a Friday, out of respect for the Passion – tradition has it that all was still on Good Friday. "Now from the sixth hour there was darkness over all the land until the ninth hour" (Matthew 27:45).

St Elmo's Fire

This is the name given to the electric light which is sometimes seen on the ends of ships' masts in rough weather. It is said to be a good omen. The phenomenon is named after the patron saint of sailors. St Elmo was Bishop of Formiae in the fourth century and was martyred by having his bowels wound out on a windlass. St Elmo's Fire is also called "corposant", from the Italian *corpo santo* ("holy body"), and St Helen's Fire. The Romans called it "Castor and Pollux" when two lights appeared (in Roman mythology the twin sons of Jupiter).

109

DISEASES AND REMEDIES

St Anthony's Fire

The complaint known as St Anthony's Fire or Sacred Fire was erysipelas (an acute infectious disease of the skin characterized by inflammation and accompanied by a fever). St Anthony the Hermit (d. AD 356), often called the founder of monasticism, relates how he was set upon by devils, who beat him so severely that it was thought he would die of his wounds. In answer to his prayers, Our Lord appeared to him and healed him. In the year 1089, when there was a plague of erysipelas in many parts of Europe, it was found that persons who implored St Anthony's prayers often obtained a cure, and from that time onward the disease was called St Anthony's Fire.

St Vitus' Dance

An extraordinary dancing madness in the fifteenth century began in Germany at Treves and Cologne and then spread into several other countries. A chapel at Ulm, dedicated to St Vitus, became a place of pilgrimage for those afflicted with this dancing mania, and this accounts for the saint's name being used to describe this curious complaint. It is now known as *chorea* (Latin for "dance"), a nervous disease which causes irregular jerking movements through involuntary muscular contractions. The victims flocked in their thousands to the chapel of St Vitus, and, in memory of this, a procession is still made yearly on Whit Tuesday to this place. St Vitus suffered martyrdom under Diocletian and his feast is kept on 15th June.

Holy wells

These were often used for cures, but today many of them have been misnamed "wishing wells" or "treacle wells". Most people think treacle wells were the invention of Lewis Carroll, but plenty of them still exist. The word "treacle" in mediaeval times meant a healing fluid, and this sense of the word was used in the Bishops' Bible of 1568 (Jeremiah 8:22: "Is there no tryacle in Gilead?"). Therefore any holy well containing water with healing properties could be said to be a treacle well. In fact the inspiration of Lewis Carroll's reference, as put in the mouth of the dormouse, was the holy well of St Frideswide at Binsey, a village neighbouring Oxford.

Friar's balsam

A remedy for wounds and ulcers made from tincture of benzoin. It was named after the friars who were the mediaeval apothecaries. Friar Lawrence in Shakespeare's *Romeo and Juliet* is an example.

The Blessing of Throats

St Blaise, Bishop of Sebaste in Cappadocia, before his execution in the persecution of the Emperor Licinius, met a child choking with a fish-bone in his throat, and miraculously cured him. This was about the year 316. Today on St Blaise's Feast Day

(3rd February) there is still performed the ritual Blessing of Throats, with two crossed candles invoking St Blaise. The custom first started in England during the fifteenth century, and was revived after the Reformation by the Rosminians at St Etheldreda's, Ely Place, London. Tradition has it that St Blaise promised that all who lit candles in his honour would have relief from any injury or disease of the throat.

CHILDREN'S GAMES AND TOYS

"Criss-Cross" (or "Chriss-Cross")

In certain children's games memories of the Catholic past have lived on. In some parts of the country children play a game which involves hopping and simultaneously pushing with one's foot a flat stone or piece of pottery into squares marked out on the ground. The game is called "Criss-Cross", which is obviously a corruption of "Christ's Cross". The term is also used in "Chriss-Cross Row" which describes a children's primer made of horn and parchment. This in turn was placed on a board with a handle for the easy use of young children. The purpose was to display the alphabet in rows, the name came from the fact that a cross occurred at the beginning and end of the rows of letters. ("You may tell it, . . . in th' Christcross row".

Endymion Porter, *Two Angry Women of Abington* (1599).

The Jack-in-the-box

This toy has a rather unfortunate history, and is still quite common. The first violent Reformers gave this title to the Blessed Sacrament, and even the Protestant government of the day objected to it, and passed a law (12th November 1547) forbidding "such vile and unseemly words". Children not long ago could obtain a well-made Jack-in-the-box with the words,

"Hocus Pocus" painted on its lid. As "Hocus Pocus" is a parody of *Hoc est Corpus*, the holy words of consecration used in the Mass, the blasphemous application of this toy to one of the greatest mysteries of the Christian faith is obvious and it is also an example of the attitude of the Reformers.

St Anne's rhyme

Children used to sing a rhyme beginning with the words:

> *Queen Anne, Queen Anne, she sits in the sun,*
> *As fair as a lily, as white as a swan . . .*

It originally began "St Anne, St Anne". No one could apply these pretty words to the rather stout and dull old lady who once reigned over us, and for whom we never seem to have had much admiration. There was a great devotion to St Anne in Catholic

England, and as her feast fell in the middle of summer (26th July) she was said to "sit in the sun". The Christian name Mary-Ann or Marian was once a favourite, as it combined Our Blessed Lady and her mother St Anne.

"Little Jack Horner"

This nursery rhyme refers to one of the famous "abbey robbers":

> *Horner, Popham and Thynne –*
> *When the monks popped out they popped in.*

Popham got Littlecote, Thynne got Longleat and Horner got the Abbey of Mells. The words, "He put in his thumb and pulled out a plum" are said to refer to the deeds of the Abbey of Mells (a plum living), which were smuggled in a pie. His descendants still own part of the Abbey but have returned to the ancient faith.

"Cat's-cradle"

This is a "cradle" made by children with a long loop of string twisted round their hands. However, the name does not seem to make much sense, as cats don't lie in cradles. The name is really "cratch-cradle". "Cratch" is the old word for a manger, so the words mean "manger-cradle". They refer to the manger at Bethlehem, which was Our Divine Lord's cradle.

PLACE NAMES

Amen Corner

This is the west end of Paternoster Row. In Catholic times, during the procession of Corpus Christi, the priests and acolytes would have completed the "Our Father" (*Pater Noster*) and said the "Amen" by the time this corner was reached. (Cf. *BDPF*)

Paternoster Row etc.

This well-known London street is said to get its name from the precursor of the rosary. It was called a paternoster and consisted of ten "Our Father" beads and one "Glory Be" bead. Wood-turners used to make these paternosters in this street. They were often of special design and were sometimes highly ornamental. There was also another Paternoster Row and a Little Paternoster Row in Spitalfields, near the former Priory of St Mary. Another theory is that the cathedral procession said the "Paternoster" along this route on Corpus Christi (see above).

Ave Maria Lane etc.

Near St Paul's in London are Ave Maria Lane, Amen Corner and Creed Lane. All of them probably date from the reign of Edward II, when the Dean and Chapter of St Paul's, finding the Cathedral precincts to be a harbour of thieves and harlots, rebuilt and purified them. (Walter Thornbury, *Old and New London* Vol.I, pub. Cassell Petter & Galpin.)

Bethlehem Hospital (or Bedlam)

Bethlehem Hospital (or Bedlam, as it was often called for short) was founded in 1247 as a hospital for lunatics, under the care of a religious order whose main house was near Bethlehem. It still exists today as a hospital for the mentally afflicted, and so it has come down from our Catholic past. In 1676 it was transferred from Bishopsgate to Moorfields in London, and in 1926 to Beckenham in Kent.

St Wilfrid's Needle

A narrow passage in the crypt of Ripon Minster built by Odo, Archbishop of Canterbury. It was said to test a woman's chastity, because none but a virgin could squeeze through.

Charing Cross

This is a well-known name that has a history beginning in 1291, when Eleanor, Queen of Edward I, was brought to Westminster Abbey for burial. The cross which was placed there was the last in a series of nine crosses that marked the Queen's coffin's journey to her grave. The name "Charing" has been said to be a corruption of la Chere Reine ("the Dear Queen"). However, there was an ancient village of Charing which stood between the City of London and Westminster. The place where Charles I's statue now stands was the site of the last of Eleanor's crosses. The other crosses were at Lincoln, Grantham, Stamford, Geddington, Northampton, Stony Stratford, Waltham and West Cheap (Cheapside). Of these crosses only those at Geddington, Northampton and Waltham now survive, Charing Cross being a Victorian reproduction.

Marylebone

The district in London which was formerly known by the infamous name of Tyburn. It was situated on the river of that name and was associated with public executions. The area was renamed Maryborne, after a church dedicated to Our Lady, but popular etymology has rendered it "Marylebone" (*BDPF*).

Blackfriars

This is now a district between Ludgate Hill and the River Thames. It derives its name from the priory of the Black (Dominican) Friars which moved to this area from Holborn in 1276. It was destroyed on the dissolution of the monasteries.

Whitefriars

A part of London extending from Fleet Street to the Thames. There was a convent of Carmelite Friars here in Catholic days. Because they wore a white religious habit they were known as the White Friars, and the district was named after them.

Greyfriars

Christ's Hospital was founded by Edward VI on the site of the Greyfriars (a Franciscan friary) in London's Newgate Street. The friary was mostly destroyed. The Franciscans were called the Grey Friars because their habits were originally of undyed wool.

Covent Garden

Most of the present parish of St Paul's (Covent Garden) was at one time the garden of Westminster Abbey. This was originally called Convent Garden, but in Elizabethan times the name was corrupted to Covent Garden.

The Court of Arches

The highest court of appeal in the old Province of Canterbury. This court met in the church of St Mary-le-bow, Cheapside, London, anciently called *Sanctae Mariae quae dicitur ad Arcus* or St Mary on the Arches (*Annales de Margam*, p. 5), after the stone arches it was built on. The court met in this Norman arched crypt before the Reformation when the only senior court was the Roman Curia. The church was destroyed in 1666 and rebuilt by Wren in 1671. The modern Court of Arches is subject to the Crown.

Clerkenwell

Clerkenwell is named after the parish Clerks' Well, dating back to the twelfth century. A holy well where the clerks would gather for their guild outing and the annual performance of miracle plays. The City Livery Guild of Parish Clerks continues today as one of the guilds of London.

Bridewell

On the western angle of the Thames, not far from Ludgate Circus, once stood Bridewell Palace, named after St Bridget's Well. Under Elizabeth I this became a prison where many Catholics languished.

The Pope's Head

This was a celebrated tavern in the reign of Edward IV and is mentioned in Samuel Pepy's *Diary*. It no longer survives but is commemorated by Pope's Head Alley off Cornhill in the City.

The Papal Crossed Keys

The insignia of the papacy derived from Christ's gift to Peter (Matthew 8: 23–27). These are commemorated by Cross Key Court in London Wall, Cross Key Square in Little Britain and Cross Key Close by Marylebone Lane.

Cardinal Cap Alley

This street is at Bankside near the former palace of the bishops of Winchester. One of those bishops, Cardinal Beaufort, is commemorated in this street name.

Bleeding Heart Yard

Bleeding Heart Yard, which is just behind Ely Place, takes its name from a nearby tavern which commemorated Our Lady of Sorrows. She was popularly depicted with seven swords piercing her heart, representing her seven sorrows.

OLD INN SIGNS

So many inn signs scattered up and down the country refer to the old religion that it is possible to give only a few samples of them. "The Lamb and Flag" and, of course, "The Agnus Dei" (the sacrificial Lamb of God bearing the banner of victory over death) are both fairly common signs with religious significance. Below are some others.

"The Salutation"

Few signs have undergone so many changes as this one. Originally it represented the angel saluting Our Blessed Lady, and this was still occasionally seen in the sixteenth and seventeenth centuries. In the time of the Commonwealth the Puritans changed it into "The Soldier and Citizen", and in this

form it continued for long after, two citizens being represented bowing politely to each other. "The Salutation Tavern" in Billingsgate has such a picture on an old trade token and so does "The Salutation Tavern" in Newgate Street. The sign is often in the form of two hands conjoined, as at "The Salutation Hotel" Perth, where a label is added with the words, "You're welcome to the city".

"The Angel"

This sign originally represented the Archangel Gabriel. Nearly all the trade tokens that carry this sign show him with scroll in his hands, and we know that the scroll contained the words he used when he spoke to Our Blessed Lady at the Annunciation. The Reformers had less objection to an angel than they had to Our Lady, so they blotted her out on their inn signs and left the angel standing. There was a famous public house with this sign at Islington. Another "Angel" still exists behind St Clement's Church in the Strand. "The Angel Inn" at Grantham, once belonging to the Knights Templars, was standing in 1213 when King John held his court there. Not quite so common is a sign called "The Flowerpot" which is connected with "The Angel". The early Reformers objected to Our Lady and the Archangel on a sign, so they painted them out. But they left the vase with the lily in it which was often shown standing between them. Then the flower went, after a time, and just the vase or flowerpot remained. So there was now nothing left to wound even the most delicate Protestant conscience.

"The Catherine Wheel"

This was another favourite sign. St Catherine was always a very popular saint, and her Feast was kept on 25th November. Legend has it that in the year 375 she was martyred at Alexandria, being condemned to be torn to pieces by wheels armed with sharp spikes. This sign was frequently changed, after the Reformation, to "The Cat and Wheel" or even to "The Clock Wheel". An example of the latter can be seen at Bristol.

"The St Blaise"

In parts of the country where wool-combers are employed, inn signs with this title may sometimes be seen. The saint was Bishop of Sebaste in Armenia and suffered martyrdom in 316, his body being torn by iron combs and hooks. He is always regarded as the special patron of those engaged in woollen trades, who use tools of this kind in their work.

"The Cardinal's Hat"

Inns at Windsor, Canterbury and several other places have the hat of a Roman Cardinal for their sign.

"St Peter's Finger"

This signs shows a right hand lifted in blessing, the two smaller fingers being folded down. The inn named "St Peter's Finger" is at Lytchett Minister, about five miles from Wareham, Dorset. Although such a sign must have been objectionable to the Reformers, as it clearly meant that it was the Pope who was giving the blessing, it has survived until the present time, and is a place where the hounds frequently meet. St Peter's name was often given to inns, and it has nearly always been changed by the Reformers to "The Cross Keys", as being less harmful.

"The Pilgrims"

Inns with this sign are generally near some celebrated shrine; Coventry and Glastonbury both have inns with this name. The pilgrims often came from far off, and needed a place of rest and refreshment.

"The Seven Stars"

A list of over twenty-five inns with this title can easily be made out, and there are many more. While it probably often referred to the constellation known as the Great Bear, it seems that it also meant the seven-starred celestial crown shown in old paintings and carvings as being worn in heaven by Our Blessed Lady.

"The Three Kings"

An inn sign that certainly takes us back to Catholic times. There was at least one inn in London, at Bucklersbury, with this sign, and it was a favourite with the silk mercers, who traded in all kinds of rich materials that they brought from Cologne.

"The Bleeding Heart"

This was the crest of the Douglas family and was often used as a sign. However, it seems that the inn of this name in Hatton Garden, London, was probably named after the Church of the Bleeding Heart, the name of which refers to the Blessed Virgin Mary (G. J. Monson-Fitzjohn, *Quaint Signs of Old Inns*, London, 1926).

FLOWERS WITH RELIGIOUS NAMES

As our wild flowers grow in country places, it is only natural that their old names would live on among simple country folk, being handed down from generation to generation. Let us take first those relating to Our Blessed Lady.

The Marigold

This plant is named in honour of Our Lady.

> *This riddle, Cuddy, if thou canst, explain . . .*
> *What flower is that which bears the virgin's name,*
> *The richest metal added to the same?*
>
> Gay, *Pastoral*

It is the symbol of goldsmiths and is still used by the bankers Child & Co.

Our Lady's Slipper
(Cypripedium calceolus)

This beautiful plant is very rare, and is only found in dense woods in Durham, Lancashire and Yorkshire. It flowers in May and June and is an Orchid. The Bird's-foot Trefoil is a pretty little yellow flower that is also called Lady's Slipper in some districts. The flowers are of a shape that easily suggests a slipper but are distinct.

Our Lady's Mantle
(Alchemilla vulgaris)

The flowers of this plant are not showy, being yellow-green and very small; its name refers to its beautiful leaves. Each leaf is large and roundish, and is cut into seven or nine lobes, which have notched edges. These lobes make a perfect little dome, as they bend downwards at their tips, and hence they suggest a mantle or covering. They are silvery beneath.

Our Lady's Smock
(Cardamine pratensis)

This is the beautiful early spring flower of which Shakespeare wrote:

> *When daisies pied, and violets blue,*
> *And Lady-smoke all silver-white . . .*
> *Do paint the meadows with delight.*

The four petals that make the flower are a very pale lilac in colour, and in some parts of the country they become double. The old leaves on the stem may dip down until they touch the ground, where they root and throw up new plants.

Our Lady's Fingers
(Anthyllis vulneraria)

This plant has rather dark bluish leaves, which are covered with silky hairs. It is not very clear why it should be called Our Lady's

Fingers, unless it is because the leaves are finger-shaped. It is so called in all old herbals.

Our Lady's Bedstraw (Galium verum)

This is often known as cleavers or goose-grass. It was largely used for strewing on floors and for laying in beds, and hence its name. It also curdles milk, and was much used in cheese-making. The stems of the plant, boiled with alum, make a useful yellow dye, and its root produces a fine red one. It was a favourite plant because it was so useful, and this probably led to its being dedicated to Our Lady.

Our Lady's Tresses (Spiranthes spiralis)

Its full title is Autumn Lady's Tresses. The plant scarcely seems to have any leaves, for they are very small and wrap closely round the flower stem. This stem is covered with a dense coat of white hairs. The top two inches of the stem make a spike of small white flowers that have a delicious scent.

Our Lady's Thistle (Carduus Marianus)

Also known as the Milk Thistle, this plant seems to be nearly world-wide. Its scientific name refers to Mary. The reason for this is the legend that during the flight into Egypt, while Mary was feeding the ass that helped in the journey, some of her milk fell upon the thistle leaves, and they have been covered ever since with the white spots and lines that are so remarkable upon this beautiful plant today.

Our Lady's Seal (Tamus communis)

This is generally called Black Bryony; it has fine heart-shaped leaves, which are very shiny. It has no hooks or tendrils to help it climb through thick hedges, but it pushes its way up and rises high above its surroundings. The small flowers produce clusters of red berries which are so like red sealing-wax that they have evidently suggested the name.

Other flowers with religious names

In addition to those flowers bearing Mary's name there are many others with names originating in Catholic times. For example, there is the Passion-flower, St John's Wort and Sweet St William, as it was called in the old herbals (it should not be confused with Sweet William, named after "Billy the Butcher", Duke of Cumberland). There is also Canterbury Bells, which are in flower at about the beginning of July. The flowers were associated with the pilgrimages being made for the great Feast of the Translation of St Thomas, the martyred Archbishop of Canterbury. This feast was held on 7th July, when the bells of the churches at Canterbury were probably very much in evidence.

We seem to have only one insect that bears a religious name, and this is the Ladybird. Its name literally means "beetle of Our Lady". It was given such a fine name because of the wonderful service it performs in eating greenfly. On the Continent its name is often closely linked with that of the Virgin Mary.

APPENDIX

The Origin of the Title "Dowry of Mary" and The Shrines of Our Lady at Westminster

(Originally a talk given to the Ecumenical Society of the Blessed Virgin Mary in September 1989.)

There is a tradition that the title "Dowry of Mary" goes back to Edward the Confessor, and yet there is no historical documentation to support this; the association of Edward with the great Abbey of Westminster is one thing, but his having any link with the Dowry tradition is quite another. The Abbey as founded (or re-founded) by Edward in 1055 was not officially associated with any such tradition, as I will endeavour to show, for about three hundred and twenty-six years. Another contention is that the Dowry tradition can be traced back to Edward III (1327–77); however, the shrine of Our Lady of the Pew, with which this tradition is associated, was already in existence in the Palace of Westminster before Edward came to the throne.

It is true that Edward refurbished the Chapel of St Stephen and rebuilt its associate Chapel of Pew in 1333, but I can find no reference to the Dowry tradition during his reign. Indeed, at this time the little Chapel of Pew (reached from St Stephen's via Edward III's Cloisters) was of no particular importance. It is known that in 1356 a College of Canons was founded to serve St Stephen's, and the Calendar of Patent Rolls (30 Edward III, p. 1) mentions the "new Collegiate Church" and the "old chapel" beside St Stephen's, which could refer to Our Lady of Pew.

The late Martin Gillett considered that the Pew Chapel was already old in Edward III's time, and that it could probably be traced back to Henry III's time as the "chapel in the King's garden" (Close Rolls, Henry III 1250–51). Edward III undoubtedly rebuilt the Pew Chapel and increased its importance, and during his reign it may well have received shrine status. In 1355 a certain Richard Lackenbury was paid £3.6s.8d. "for a certain image of St Mary" (Martin Gillett's unpublished notes). This may refer to the shrine statue, for in 1369 a priest named John Bulwyk was given a grant for life to celebrate divine service before the image of Blessed Mary "in La Piewe" (the Pew Chapel) by the King's Chapel of St Stephen within the Palace of Westminster (Close Rolls, Edward III 1367–70).

The origins of the name "pew" are obscure, but there is good reason for associating it with the French *puissant* ("powerful"), as it was common to anglicize French words, and an Englishman would probably pronounce this word as "pewssant" anyway. Moreover, there is the association of the French shrine of Our Lady of Le Puy, and if, as some contend, the Latin *podium* ("strong support") is the origin, the connection with the hill shrine of Le Puy as a strong-point further connects with the idea of power, and with Our Lady's title *Virgo Potens*.

So far we have considered the Palace shrine, but more familiar to us today is the shrine in the Abbey Church. There had in fact been two shrines of Our Lady of Pew from the last quarter of the fourteenth century until the Reformation. The Palace shrine, rebuilt after a fire in 1452, survived the Reformation, but was finally destroyed by fire in 1834. The Abbey shrine was established in an unprecedented way. The Chapel of Henry VII being the original Lady Chapel (in the apse beyond the high altar), the little shrine which has now become the focus of attention began with a widow's benefaction for the soul of her husband. The Countess of Pembroke (whose husband Aylmer de Valence, Earl of Pembroke, has a fine effigy in the Chapel of SS Edmund and Thomas) established a mortuary chapel for daily Masses for her husband next to the Chapel of St John, and she presented the Abbot of Westminster with an alabaster statue of Our Lady. This is probably how the Abbey chapel came to be, because the monks of Westminster had just lost a battle with the canons of St Stephen's with regard to ecclesiastical jurisdiction in the Palace of Westminster, and thus were debarred from the Palace shrine of Our Lady of Pew. The Abbot therefore apparently lost no time in establishing with the Countess' gift a secondary shrine of Pew which, unlike the other, with its restriction to courtiers, would be accessible to all. The Countess'

will, proved in 1377, records that the statue of Our Lady was already in position at the secondary shrine of Pew. And, according to the Sacrist's Roll of 1378–80, the image of the Blessed Mary called "Le Puwe" was already much in evidence.

At this point I wish to concentrate on the shrine of Our Lady of Pew, with its fine alabaster statue, as it is known today, the cause of not inconsiderable religious initiative and inspiration. This shrine, I would suggest, has proved the more important of the two, and it is here that we must look for the origins of England's title, "Dowry of Mary".

In 1955 a benefactor, who wished to remain anonymous, commissioned Sister Concordia Stuart of Minster Abbey on the Isle of Thanet to carve a statue of Our Lady to replace the one lost from the Pew Chapel at the Reformation. I corresponded with Sister Concordia at the time, explaining that she was probably replacing a statue that was first associated with the title *Dos Mariae*. This description of England as "Mary's Dowry" moreover suggested an occasion of ecumenical initiative – of seeking unity once more – through Mary. Like the original statue presented by the Countess, the new one had to be in English alabaster, which was hard to obtain in the required measurements (3 feet by 16 inches by 7 inches), as the model for the work was to be the statue of Our Lady of Westminster in Westminster Cathedral (a fifteenth-century English carving of the Nottingham school).

To this statue, though it has no historical connection with the Pew Chapel, has been ascribed the title *Virgo Potens*, "Our Lady of Power". Thus there is perhaps an incidental connection in the dedication of the two Madonnas. The statue in Westminster Cathedral found its way back to England via the Paris Exhibition of 1954, where the scholar S. W. Wolsey spotted it. Through his efforts and the munificence of an anonymous benefactor, it was restored to the Church and enshrined in Westminster Cathedral in 1955. On 10th May 1971 a similar ceremony took place in Westminster Abbey, when the statue which Sister Concordia had carved, based on the one in Westminster Cathedral, was placed in the Pew Chapel, in a niche that had been empty since the Reformation. This was a splendidly ecumenical occasion, made possible by the Dean of Westminster Abbey, and it forged a link between the two great churches of Westminster. On the back of the statue Sister Concordia had carved *UT UNUM SINT* ("That they may be one").

It is not certain what the original statue of Our Lady of Pew looked like, but an inspection of the shrine chapel will give some clues. In 1896 Sir Gilbert Scott was conducting repairs in the Chapel of St John the Baptist, to which the Pew Chapel gives access, when his pupil, John Mickelthwaite, made an interesting discovery. In the Pew Chapel, with the benefit of extra light, he found a boss in the ceiling depicting the Assumption of Our Lady, and against the wall a bracket and an iron fitting which he deduced had supported the original shrine statue. Against the north wall he also discovered a painted nimbus or aureole of light still plainly visible, which must originally have surrounded the image of Our Lady. From the size and shape of this aureole, it would seem reasonable to suppose that the original statue was a standing one, and, from the style of the vaulting and decoration, Mickelthwaite concluded that the whole work could be dated around 1380. This date is of particular importance in establishing the Dowry tradition.

It was in 1381 that England was ravaged by the Peasants' Revolt, when the imposition of a poll tax caused the south-eastern counties to rise in open rebellion. Froissart's *Chronicles* gives a vivid description of how the young King Richard II prepared to meet the rebels, under Wat Tyler, at Smithfield:

Richard II on the Saturday after Corpus Christi went to Westminster, where he heard Mass at the Abbey with all his Lords. He made his devotions at a statue of Our Lady in a little chapel that had witnessed many miracles and where much grace had been gained, so that the Kings of England have much faith in it.

Another chronicler, Strype, described the event as follows:

On the coming of the rebels and Wat Tyler, the same King went to Westminster . . . confessed himself to an anchorite; then took himself to the chapel of Our Lady of Pew; there he said his devotions, and went to Smithfield to meet the rebels.

From this and other evidence, we learn that the Pew Chapel had already been in existence for some time before Richard II's reign.

So what Mickelthwaite discovered in the Pew Chapel in 1869, and dated around 1380, must have been a refurbishment of the shrine. What, therefore, was the situation which occasioned Richard II's re-ordering of the shrine? In the answer to this question lies the clue to the origin of England's title, *Dos Mariae*, "Mary's Dowry".

The original shrine, as we know, was housed in a chapel within the Palace of Westminster attached to the Collegiate Church of St Stephen. This shrine survived the Reformation, but, as I have explained, was finally destroyed in the fire of 1843. Today its exact location may be determined by the site of the Speaker's House next to the now restored Church of St Stephen. It was at this greater shrine that the sovereigns of England were wont to beseech the help of Our Lady, but the little chapel in the Abbey survives with evidence to show that it was patronized by at least one sovereign in particular.

The Abbey shrine is probbly more significant as evidence for England's title, *Dos Mariae*, as its existence as a shrine dates from the time of Richard's successful bid to keep his throne, and it is probably a grateful monarch's gift to his people who did not have access to the greater shrine within the Palace. Moreover, the traces of painting on the walls of this little chapel are irrefutable evidence of King Richard's patronage, as there are on the east wall remnants of the King's "white hart" badge. Therefore, what was originally a chantry chapel, the King by all accounts transformed into a public shrine dedicated to Our Lady of Pew. This was the lesser shrine, but perhaps the more significant, as its foundation marked the gratitude of King Richard to Our Lady for the safe return of his realm, in offering it to her as her dowry.

A search for clues must perforce include the examination of what ecclesiastical *objets d'art* have survived from this period of Richard's reign, especially those specifically associated with the monarch. The one noteable example is, of course, the Wilton Diptych, housed today in the National Gallery. As to the origin of this Diptych, a theory was first put forward by the late Everard Green, Rouge Dragon Pursuivant of the College of Arms. He held that it was a votive offering made to the (greater) shrine of Our Lady of Pew on the occasion of Richard's coronation in 1371. W. G. Constable wrote in 1929 concerning this theory as follows:

> The king is known to have visited this shrine shortly after that ceremony, and to have made a special offering there. It is suggested that the eleven angels [on the Diptych] wearing the King's badges, of a white hart, and of a collar and pendant of peascods, stand for the age of the King at the time of his coronation (eleven years) or could also be his monetary offering of eleven "angels" ("angel" as a monetary unit apparently not having come into use until Richard's reign). The red-cross banner [being offered to Our Lady in the Diptych] Green regarded as an offering to the Virgin to symbolize England being the *Dos Mariae*, as described in a mandate of Archbishop Arundel. ("The Date and Nationality of the Wilton Diptych", *The Burlington Magazine*, No. CCCXVI, Vol. LV.) Cf. Sir Martin Conway, *The Times*, 26th June 1929, p. 17.

This mandate, at the special desire of the King, was issued at Lambeth on 10th February 1399, and reads as follows:

> The contemplation of the great mystery of the Incarnation has brought all Christian nations to venerate her from whom came the beginnings of redemption. But we, as the humble servants of her inheritance, and liegemen of her especial dower – as we

are approved by common parlance – ought to excel all others in the favour of our praises and devotions to her.

Everard Green's suggestion that the red-cross banner in the Wilton Diptych symbolizes England's being the *Dos Mariae* has not so far been substantiated. However, a closer examination of the evidence which connects the Diptych with the Pew Chapel will help to prove his point.

A study of the sequence of events surrounding the young King Richard's meeting with the rebels will help to show the significance of the red-cross banner. This banner was that of St George, and it therefore represented the Kingdom of England. The rebels had produced their own standards under which they marched to London, but, upon meeting with the young King at Blackheath and then at Smithfield, they were finally persuaded to tear down their own standards and accept the standard of the realm which the King was carrying. To return to Froissart's *Chronicles*, this event can be dated approximately to 15th June 1381. After his success in quelling the rebels, and their acceptance of the standard of the realm, Richard returned to meet his mother at Westminster and to give thanks. Froissart records the young King's words as follows:

> "Yes, Madam . . . rejoice and praise God, for today I have regained my kingdom which I had lost."
> And he placed the Kingdom under Our Lady's protection – in thanksgiving for having regained it.

When Mickelthwaite dated the Pew Chapel around 1380, he was influenced by subsequent refurbishing for which King Richard was undoubtedly responsible. The occasion of the refurbishing must have been in thanksgiving for the quelling of the Peasants' Revolt, and therefore 1381 would seem to be a more accurate date. The evidence for this and for the connection with the Wilton Diptych will all help to establish the tradition of Our Lady's Dowry.

The decoration in the Pew Chapel includes an incomplete survival on the east wall of the "white hart" badge of Richard II, which must be compared with the similar badges on the angels in the Wilton Diptych.

To the right of the shrine is a pillar whose capital bears a shield displaying the cross of St George; this no doubt has some connection with the red-cross banner in the Diptych in representing England as Mary's Dower. This Chapel of Pew provides an entrance to the Chapel of St John the Baptist, and in the Diptych St John the Baptist is shown commending King Richard to Our Lady. In a line south from the Chapel of St John the Baptist, behind the High Altar, is the shrine of St Edward the Confessor, and next to this is the Chapel of St Edmund, King and Martyr. These two saints likewise appear commending King Richard to Our Lady in the Wilton Diptych. This would appear to establish the connection of the Diptych with this Pew Chapel, and it was most likely presented to the shrine by Richard in thanksgiving for the safe return of his realm. In the Diptych Our Lady is shown accepting the standard of England in token of her dowry.

The figure of Mary in the Diptych probably most accurately represents the original shrine statue, as has been ascertained from the painted aureole, which indicates a standing figure.

The historian F. Alfad (alias Griffiths, SJ), writing before the French troops sacked Rome in 1798, stated that in his time at the English College in Rome there existed, although since destroyed, an ancient painting of a King and Queen who, on their knees, were making an offering of England to Our Blessed Lady for her dower through the hands of John the Baptist, with this inscription: *Dos tua pia laec ese, quare leges, Maria*. A rough translation of the rather obscure Latin begins: "This is your dowry, pious Virgin . . ." (Edmund Waterton, FSA, *Pietas Mariana Britannica*, (1879, pp. 11–17). This surely was a portrait of Richard II and his consort, Ann of Bohemia. The attitude in which they are represented would certainly seem to commemorate an offering of the English realm to Our Blessed Lady as her dowry. In the British Library (Harl. MS no.360) there is further evidence of this ancient painting; the manuscript, from the reign of James I, reads as follows:

> In the Church of Saint Thomas Hospitall in Roome [the original name for the English College] there is a very faire painted and guilded Table of Imagerie works, standing before the Altars of Saint Edmund the martire, once a King of England; . . . It is in length abooue five foote, and about three foote high.

The manuscript goes on to describe a young king kneeling before the Lady and holding between his hands a "patterne of words, *Dos tua Virgo pia Haec est*" ("This is your dowry, O pious Virgin").

Archbishop Arundel's mandate of 1399 described England as *"Dos Mariae* in common parlance" by the fourteenth century, and the manuscript of James I's time declares that "it is no new devised speech to call England Our Ladyes dowerie". I would suggest that the title was obtained not so much by special devotion as by the solemn consecration that King Richard II made of the English realm to Mary as her Dowry on the Saturday after Corpus Christi in the eventful year of 1381.